To Dad
Happy Christma~
With love
from

DISCOVER YOUR
CHESS
STRENGTH

INTERNATIONAL GRANDMASTER
RAYMOND KEENE

An Owl Book
Henry Holt and Company
New York

Library of Congress Catalog Card Number: 92-54270

ISBN 0-8050-2432-8 (An Owl Book: pbk.)

Henry Holt books are available at special discounts
for bulk purchases for sales promotions, premiums,
fund-raising, or educational use. Special editions
or book excerpts can also be created to specification.

For details contact: Special Sales Director,
Henry Holt and Company, Inc., 115 West 18th Street,
New York, New York 10011.

First American Edition—1992

Printed in the United Kingdom
Recognizing the importance of preserving
the written word, Henry Holt and Company, Inc.,
by policy, prints all of its first editions
on acid-free paper. ∞

10   9   8   7   6   5   4   3   2   1

Advisor: R. D. Keene GM, OBE
Technical Editor: Andrew Kinsman

Contents

Algebraic Notation

The moves contained in this book are given in what is known as 'Figurine Algebraic Notation'. This somewhat complicated sounding term actually describes a very simple way of writing down the moves. Readers familiar with the system can jump ahead to the games themselves, but those who are comparatively new to the game or who have only learned the older English Descriptive notation will find what follows helpful. It is assumed that the reader already knows how to *play* chess.

Each piece is represented by a symbol, called a 'Figurine', as follows:

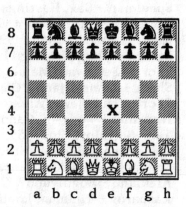

Pawn	♙
Knight	♘
Bishop	♗
Rook	♖
Queen	♕
King	♔

The squares on the chessboard are described by coordinates, consisting of a letter followed by a number (see diagram). For instance the square marked with a cross is called 'e4'. This follows exactly the same principle as reading off a reference on an A–Z street guide or road map. Everybody can pick this up in a matter of minutes. There is no mystery to it at all!

Introduction

Chessplayers love statistics and are particularly fasci-
nated with questions such as, who was the greatest
player of all time? This love of statistical evaluation can
be observed, if by no other means, from the fact that the
World Chess Federation (FIDE) issues a twice yearly
ranking list containing thousands of names, each with a
numerical ranking based on the mathematical theories of
Professor Arpad Elo. On Professor Elo's scale approx-
imately 2700 represents world championship level, 2600
world championship candidate standard, 2500 grandmaster and 2400 international master.

The World Chess Federation Ratings Commission has
issued some fascinating figures showing *peak* ratings
throughout the history of chess.

Leading ELO/FIDE ratings

Gary Kasparov	USSR	2800
Bobby Fischer	USA	2785
Anatoly Karpov	USSR	2755
Vassily Ivanchuk	USSR	2735
José Capablanca	Cuba	2725
Mikhail Botvinnik	USSR	2720
Emanuel Lasker	Germany	2720
Mikhail Tal	USSR	2705
Boris Gelfand	USSR	2700
Viktor Korchnoi	USSR/Switzerland	2695
Alexander Alekhine	Russia/France	2690
Boris Spassky	USSR/France	2690
Nigel Short	England	2685

It is clear that Kasparov, Fischer and Karpov are the contenders for the top three slots but it is tragic that Fischer's self-imposed reclusiveness has deprived us of any games by him at all against either of the two great Russians. Fischer became the highest-rated player of all-time before retiring, but Kasparov has since deposed him.

However, an even more burning statistical question for most chess players is:

What is my own rating?

For the elite who are playing constantly in official tournaments, this question is not a problem. National and international chess bodies are constantly issuing updated rating lists giving new evaluations of the most active players' chess strengths.

But, for the home chess enthusiast, or the player who simply does not have time to compete in official chess tournaments, or who is so busy in his or her professional life that the only games possible are those with a chess computer, the question: What is my chess rating? is considerably more difficult.

This book is designed to answer that question.

It contains 20 carefully annotated games, played by the world's best chessplayers. At key points, each of which is marked clearly with a diagram, a test question is asked, enabling points to be scored which correspond exactly with the points available on international and national chess rating scales. (There will also be bonuses on offer for finding particularly tricky or difficult variations. Watch out very closely for such opportunities to maximise your points score!) Your score in this book will not automatically entitle you to such a rating, but it will show the potential the reader can achieve, if he or she ventures forth into competitive junior or senior chess. For parents, if you think you have a chess prodigy on your hands, this book can also be the fastest way to find out. If you are ambitious, then this book is the indispensable teaching tool to help you to progress towards master strength, or a FIDE international rating.

Before passing on to the main body of games, here are the rating scores possible in tabular form translated into the systems used by the World and US Chess Federations and the British Chess Federation.

Explanation of Chess Ratings

A	B	C
2800	275	Gary Kasparov (World Record Rating)
2700	263	World Champion
2600	250	World Championship Candidate
2500	238	Grandmaster
2400	225	International master/US Senior master
2300	213	FIDE master
2200	200	US Life Master
2000	175	International FIDE-rated player
1800	150	Class A Strong club player
1600	125	Class B Medium club player
1400	100	Class C Home computer player
1200	75	Class D Experienced social player
1000	50	Social player
1000-	50-	Keep reading *The Times* chess column for practice.

A) ELO ratings, as used by the World and US Chess Federations

B) British Chess Federation equivalent rating

C) Title

Self-Improvement Graph

As you go through the book progressively fill in your score for each game.

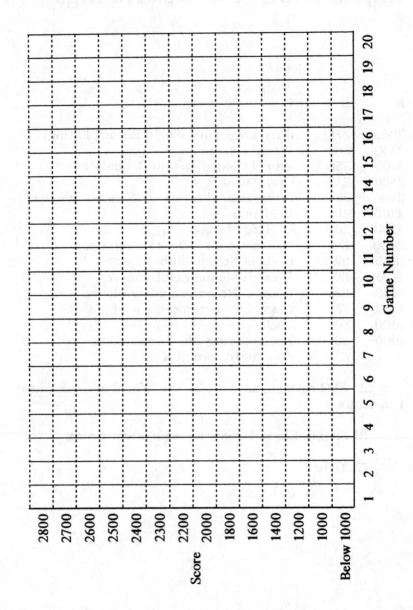

McNab - Wojtkiewicz
Hastings Challengers 1989/90
English Opening

Your Target: 2400 points

Your partner is Scottish international master Colin McNab. You have the white pieces and your opponent is Alex Wojtkiewicz from Poland.

You will be posed a series of questions during this game each of which is announced by a diagram. Points will be awarded for the correct answer. The maximum amount of points available for this game is 2400, equivalent to an international master. At each diagram where a question is posed you may use your own discretion to award yourself 100 points if you do not find the move played but choose instead any other move that does not allow your opponent to capture material for no compensation or to checkmate you. For each diagram question, you may always use your discretion to award yourself 100 points for your chosen move unless there are clear instructions to the contrary.

As you play through the game use a sheet of paper to cover the page so that the test move under each diagram is not prematurely revealed.

1	c4	c5
2	♘f3	♘f6
3	g3	b6
4	♗g2	♗b7
5	d3	e6
6	e4	d6

Black has chosen the resilient Hedgehog Defence. His strategy is to erect a defensive wall of spines with pawns on a6, b6, d6 and e6. Behind this wall Black will defy White to launch an attack.

7	0–0	♗e7

	8 ♘c3	0-0

It is sensible for Black to castle his king into safety as early as possible.

	9 b3	a6

An unassuming move which prepares to bring the black queen to c7 without being botheres by ♘b5 from White. Black is basing his play on the assumption that White will eventually sacrifice a tempo with d3 - d4 to reach a normal Hedgehog.

	10 ♗b2	♛c7
	11 ♖c1	♖e8

Now examine the diagram and try to guess White's next move. Follow the same procedure throughout the rest of the game.

	12 ♖e1

200 points. More or less announcing that he is going to play d4. The alternative would be to leave the white rook on f1 and steer for f4 followed by f5 and g4. This plan could perhaps have been introduced via 12 ♘h4 freeing the white f-pawn. *200 points* if you chose 12 ♘h4 instead of 12 ♖e1.

	12 ...	♘bd7
	13 d4	cxd4
	14 ♘xd4	♖ad8

This move does not fit into a Hedgehog formation. Traditionally the black queen's rook should go to c8. The d6-pawn has plenty of protection in any case and, as we shall see, on d8 the rook is exposed to attack. It does though take play of a high order of imagination to exploit this fact.

Now, what did White play?

15 f4

250 points. If White is to make progress he must gain space on the kingside, with a view to a future attack in that sector.

15 ... ♗f8

Now, how did White proceed?

16 g4

300 points. A remarkably self-confident decision, which might have rebounded on White's own structure. This move and White's next are designed to force Black to react to the threat of g5 and thereby loosen the pawns around his king.

16 ... g6

This defensive move creates an anchor for the black knight to go to h5.

17 ♗f3

Renewing the threat of g5, harassing the black knight on f6.

17 ... h6

What is White's next move?

18 ♘d5

550 points. A superb sacrifice. Black has to accept, but in short order both his king and his queen come under fire.

18	...	exd5
19	cxd5	♛b8
20	♘c6	

Now we see why the placing of the black rook on d8 was unfortunate. Black cannot recapture on c6 without ruinous loss of material.

20	...	♛a8

Not 20 ... ♗xc6 21 dxc6 with the threat of 22 c7.
What did White play now?

21 e5

300 points. White quite correctly eschews the immediate capture of Black's rook on d8. First he sets in motion a murderous mass of central pawns.

21	...	dxe5
22	fxe5	♘h7
23	♘xd8	♛xd8

How should White continue his attack?

24 e6

200 points. It is vitally important to come to direct grips with the black king and blast him out of his corner fortress.

        24 ...   ♘df6

        25 exf7+

McNab sacrifices the potential for promotion in the interests of stripping away the pawn protection from Black's king. Both players here were in time trouble.

        25 ...   ♔xf7

        26 ♖xe8   ♘xe8

        27 ♕e2   ♗c8

It looks as if White's attack should be slowing down, now that he has traded in some pressure for material. Perhaps Black should defend the e6-square with ... ♘g5. In any case, after the text there is a resurgence of White's initiative. In particular White's queen is extremely mobile and there are tasty targets on both sides of the board.

What is White's next move?

28 ♕c4

200 points. The best square for the queen preparing to invade the black position on either wing.

28	...	♘g5
29	♗g2	♘d6
30	♕d4	♕e7
31	♖f1+	♔e8
32	♕xb6	♗xg4

White can pick up another pawn here with 33 ♕xa6, but is this the best move?

33 ♗a3

250 points. This is the most incisive. It carries the tremendous threat of 34 ♖xf8+.

33	...	♘gf7
34	♗b4	♕b7
35	♖e1+	♗e7

How does White finish off?

36 ♕xb7

150 points. Simple enough, but this move signals the end of Black's resistance. In the time scramble Black loses all of his pieces.

36	...	♘xb7
37	♖xe7+	♔d8
38	♖xb7	♘e5
39	♗a5+	♔c8
40	♖c7+	♔b8
41	d6	1-0

You should keep a record of your points scored on the table below so that you can add them up at the end of this book and calculate your exact chess strength.

Your points for this game.
Tick one of these:

2400	☐	1600+	☐
2300+	☐	1400+	☐
2200+	☐	1200+	☐
2000+	☐	1000+	☐
1800+	☐	less than 1000	☐

2 J. Polgar - Knaak
Cologne 1990
French Defence

Your Target: 2500 points

Your partner is the amazing Hungarian teenage girl prodigy Judith Polgar, who is one of the most exciting
players of modern times. You have the white pieces and
your opponent is Rainer Knaak, the German grandmaster.

You will be posed a series of questions during this
game each one of which is announced by a diagram. Points
will be awarded for the correct answer and there will also
be bonus points available for seeing correctly into difficult variations. The maximum amount of points available
for this game is 2500, equivalent to a grandmaster. At
each diagram where a question is posed (but not in the
bonus variations) you may use your own discretion to
award yourself 100 points if you do not find the move
played but choose instead any other move that does not
allow your opponent to capture material for no compensation or to checkmate you. For each diagram question,
you may always use your discretion to award yourself 100
points for your chosen move unless there are clear instructions to the contrary.

As you play through the game use a sheet of paper to
cover the page so that the test move under each diagram
is not prematurely revealed.

1	e4	e6
2	d4	d5
3	♘c3	♗b4

The Winawer system in the French Defence, one of the
sharpest and most volatile of modern openings.

4	e5	c5
5	a3	♗xc3+
6	bxc3	♘e7

7 ♕g4 ♛c7

A well-known variation of the French Defence has arisen. White normally plays now 8 ♕xg7 ♜g8 9 ♕xh7 cxd4 10 ♘e2, sacrificing the initiative in the interests of gaining material. This is, however, not in Judith's style. Spurning material she strives for the attack herself.

Now examine the diagram and try to guess White's next move. Follow the same procedure throughout the rest of the game.

8 ♗d3

Just *150 points* for this after the clue which I gave.

8 ... cxd4

Nigel Short has preferred the blockading move 8 ... c4 at this stage, which is probably an improvement, e.g. Bellin - Short, British Ch. 1987 9 ♗e2 ♘f5 10 ♘f3 ♗d7 11 ♘h4 ♜g8 12 ♘xf5 exf5 13 ♕h3 h6 14 ♕g3 ♛c6 15 ♗h5 ♛e6. Black won in 43 moves.

9 ♘e2 ♛xe5

A very risky pawn snatch.
Now, what did White play?

10 ♗f4

150 points. Introducing the theme of attack on the dark squares. If you follow this thematic concept throughout the rest of this game you will not go far wrong. Now think carefully as there is a bonus coming soon.

	10	...	♕f6
	11	♗g5	♕e5
	12	cxd4	h5

The point of the move played is to drive White's queen from the g-file. Instead 12 ... ♕c7 13 ♗f4 ♕d8 14 ♕xg7 ♖g8 15 ♕xh7 ♖xg2 16 ♗g3 followed by ♔f1 would be dreadful for Black. Give yourself a *200 point bonus* for seeing this.

What did White play now?

13 ♕h4

200 points. Not 13 dxe5 hxg4 when Black's problems will have melted away. No points if you played 13 dxe5.

	13	...	♕c7
	14	♗f4	♕a5+
	15	♗d2	♕d8

How should White continue the attack?

16 g4

400 points and a bonus coming. Judith displays commendable energy in prosecuting her attack. Black's most prudent defence would now be 16 ... ♘g6, though after 17 ♕xd8+ ♔xd8 18 gxh5 ♖xh5 19 ♗xg6 fxg6 20 ♘f4 ♖h6 21 0-0-0 ♘c6 22 c3 g5 23 ♘d3 ♖g6 24 ♖dg1 g4 25 ♘f4 White retains the advantage. Up to *200 bonus points* depending on how much of this you saw.

| | 16 ... | e5 |
| | 17 dxe5 | ♗xg4 |

What did White play now?

18 ♖g1

200 points. It is admirable to see how rapidly White's attacking units enter the game. What is Black's best defence?

| | 18 ... | ♕d7 |

After the game the players agreed that the best here for Black would have been 18 ... ♘g6 19 ♕g3 ♕h4 20 ♕e3 ♘c6 21 0-0-0. *150 bonus points* for seeing this.

| | 19 f3 | ♗e6 |

Seeking to shore up his defences. 19 ... ♗xf3 20 ♖xg7 is extremely dangerous but perhaps 19 ... ♗f5, offering to exchange some pieces, would have been somewhat better.

	20 ♘d4	♘bc6
	21 ♘xc6	♘xc6
	22 ♖xg7	

Now think very carefully about Black's possible defences. There is a bonus coming.

| | 22 ... | ♕c7 |

Black's king is pinned in the centre but White's pawn on e5 still represents a source of weakness. Knaak's 22nd move actually contains a clever point but Judit has seen further. If instead 22 ... ♘xe5 23 ♕g3 ♘xd3+ 24 cxd3 ♖c8 25 ♗b4 ♕b5 26 ♕g5 ♖c7 27 ♔d2 with the powerful threat of ♖c1. Alternatively 23 ... ♘c6 24 ♖g8+ ♔e7 25 ♗g5+ f6 26 ♗xf6+ ♔xf6 27 ♕g5+ with mate to follow. Award yourself up to *200 bonus points* for this. Now, what did White play?

23 f4

150 points. Seemingly obvious as a defence of the e5-pawn but you had to take Black's next move into account when you decided on this move. Otherwise just take *100 points*.

23 ... ♘xe5

The clever point of Black's defence, but it turns out to be inadequate.

24 fxe5 ♕xe5+

How did White parry the check?

25 ♔f2

In fact this move is obvious and forced so there are no points on offer for it, but think about what happens now if Black captures the rook on a1. There will be a bonus for

this! This is most interesting namely 25 ... ♕xa1 26 ♘b4
♚d7 27 ♖xf7+ ♗xf7 28 ♕e7+ ♚c6 29 ♘b5+ ♚xb5 30 ♕c5+
♚a6 31 ♕a5 mate. Up to *150 bonus points* depending on
how much of this you saw.

	25	...	♕xg7
	26	♖g1	♕b2
	27	♘b4	f6

What should White play to keep Black pinned down?

28 ♖e1

150 points. Now consider how Black might defend his
position, a bonus is coming.

28 ... 0-0-0

Essentially capitulation since Black is now hopelessly
behind on material but if 28 ... ♚f7 29 ♖xe6 ♚xe6 30 ♕h3+
♚f7 31 ♕d7+ ♚g8 32 ♕xd5+ ♚g7 33 ♕d7+ and mate follows.
200 bonus points for this.

29	♖xe6	♚b8
30	♕xf6	♕a2
31	♕d4	♖c8
32	♘d2	♚a8
33	♘e3	♖xc2+
34	♘xc2	♕xc2+
35	♚e1	♕b1+
36	♚d2	♕a2+
37	♚d1	♕b1+
38	♚e2	♕c2+
39	♘d2	♖f8
40	♕xd5	1-0 Black lost on time

You should keep a record of your points scored on the
table below so that you can add them up at the end of

this book and calculate your exact chess strength.

Your points for this game.
Tick one of these:

2500	☐	1600+	☐
2400+	☐	1400+	☐
2300+	☐	1200+	☐
2200+	☐	1000+	☐
2000+	☐	less than 1000	☐
1800+	☐		

3

Wolff - Flear
London 1990
Ruy Lopez

Your Target: 2500 points

Your partner is American grandmaster Patrick Wolff. You have the white pieces and your opponent is the British grandmaster Glenn Flear.

You will be posed a series of questions during this game each one of which is announced by a diagram. Points will be awarded for the correct answer and there will also be bonus points available for seeing correctly into difficult variations. The maximum amount of points available for this game is 2500, equivalent to a grandmaster. **This game is so sharp and there are so many "only moves" played that there is no dispensation on this occasion to receive 100 points for moves that are not mentioned.**

As you play through the game use a sheet of paper to cover the page so that the test move under each diagram is not prematurely revealed.

1	e4	e5
2	♘f3	♘c6
3	♗b5	a6
4	♗a4	♘f6
5	0-0	♘xe4

Temporarily winning a pawn, but it cannot be held.

6	d4	b5
7	♗b3	d5

Black must give back the pawn. If he tries to be greedy with 7 ... exd4 then 8 ♖e1 d5 9 ♘c3 ♗e6 10 ♘xe4 dxe4 11 ♖xe4 ♗e7 12 ♗xe6 fxe6 13 ♘xd4 and White has the advantage, Fischer – Trifunovic, Bled 1961.

8	dxe5	♗e6
9	♘bd2	♘c5
10	c3	d4

11   ♘g5

This ingenious sacrifice was first seen in the game Karpov - Korchnoi (10) 1978 World Championship at Baguio.
Korchnoi declined the knight and drew with difficulty.
A word of advice here. You should keep searching for critical variations for both sides at all times during this
game. This game is extremely sharp and ultra-tactical and
you must be continually thinking in advance in terms of
concrete variations.

11   ...   ♛xg5

Now examine the diagram and try to guess White's next
move. Follow the same procedure throughout the rest of
the game.

12   ♛f3

200 points for this. You should now be thinking about
which line might constitute Black's best defence. There is
a huge bonus coming if you get this right.

12   ...   ♗d7

Flear is intending to follow a recommendation for
Black in the five-volume Yugoslav *Encyclopaedia of Chess
Openings.* Nevertheless, Wolff is ready with an improvement on published theory. The safest defence for Black is
12 ... 0-0-0 13 ♛xc6 ♛xe5 14 ♘f3 ♛d5! 15 ♗xd5 ♗xd5 trapping White's queen and leading to equality. The key reference in this variation is Smyslov - Timman, European
Club Championship 1979: 13 ♗xe6+ fxe6 14 ♛xc6 ♛xe5 15
b4 ♛d5 16 ♛xd5 exd5 17 bxc5 dxc3 18 ♘b3 d4 which is
regarded as leading to dynamic equality. Award yourself a
bonus of up to *500 points* depending on how much of this
you saw while trying to work out Black's best defence.

13   ♗xf7+   ♔e7

Now, what did White play?

14   &d5

200 points for this.

14	...	&xe5
15	♕e2	d3
16	♕e1	c6
17	f4	♕h6

Now White played a real star move. What was it? There is also a bonus in the air, so think very carefully!

18   &f3!

500 points for this move. A theoretical novelty and better than the established line 18 ♕xe5+ (*200* if you chose this move) 18 ... ♔d8 19 &f3 &d6 when Black has counterplay. If now 18 ... ♕xf4 19 &xc6 leaves Black in all sorts of trouble. *100 bonus points* if you saw this. The point of White's 18th move is to be able to capture on e5 with the pawn rather than the queen. This has the effect both of liberating White's queen's bishop and of adding a central battering ram to White's attacking resources.

18   ...   ♔d8

19 fxe5

Now we can see with full clarity the point behind White's innovation. He has a dangerous passed pawn in the centre which Black has to blockade. In contrast Black's own passed pawn on d3 is too far flung and liable to be rounded up at any minute.

	19	...	♗e7
	20	♘b3	♕g6
	21	♘d4	♔c7
	22	b4	♘e6

What is White's next move?

23 ♗e4

200 points for this. Once again, since a bonus is coming, you should now be thinking carefully about Black's best defence.

23 ...   ♘xd4

Part of the charm of this game resides in Black's fiercely ingenious efforts to defend. If now 24 ♗xg6 ♘e2+ 25 ♔h1 hxg6 with the threat of ... ♖xh2+ and ... ♖h8+. *300 bonus points* if you saw this. Unfortunately for Flear, White can ignore this demonstration and instead proceed with his offensive against the black king.

24 cxd4   ♗xb4

Black continues with an ingenuity born of desperation. Any other move would lose the pawn on d3 for no compensation. Now though, Flear becomes desperately weak on the dark squares around his exposed king.

	25	♕xb4	♕xe4
	26	♕d6+	♔c8
	27	♗d2	♖e8

White's best now is?

28 ♖f7

200 points for this.

28	...	♖a7
29	♖c1	♖e6
30	♖f8+	♖e8

How does White administer the *coup de grâce*?

31 e6!

200 points. This terminates Black's resistance in most elegant fashion. If now 31 ... ♗xe6 32 ♖xe8+ or 31 ... ♕xe6 32 ♖xc6+ ♗xc6 33 ♕xe6+ or in this line 32 ... ♔b7 33 ♖b6+ ♔a8 34 ♕b8+ ♖xb8 35 ♖bxb8 mate. *100 bonus points* if you saw all of this.

31	...	♖xf8
32	exd7+	♔b7
33	d8(♕)	♖xd8
34	♕xd8	1-0

You should keep a record of your points scored on the table below so that you can add them up at the end of this book and calculate your exact chess strength.

Your points for this game.
Tick one of these:

2500 ☐			1600+ ☐	
2400+ ☐			1400+ ☐	
2300+ ☐			1200+ ☐	
2200+ ☐			1000+ ☐	
2000+ ☐		less than 1000	☐	
1800+ ☐				

Kamsky - Tal
New York Open 1990
King's Indian Defence

Your Target: 2500 points

Your partner is the teenage US grandmaster Gata Kamsky, formerly of the USSR before he defected at the tender age of 15, who has now risen to become Olympic top board for the USA. You have the white pieces and your opponent is Mikhail Tal, world champion from 1960 to 1961.

You will be posed a series of questions during this game each of which is announced by a diagram. Points will be awarded for the correct answer and there will also be bonus points available for seeing correctly into difficult variations. The maximum amount of points available for this game is 2500, equivalent to a grandmaster. At each diagram where a question is posed (but not in the bonus variations) you may use your own discretion to award yourself 100 points if you do not find the move played but choose instead any other move that does not allow your opponent to capture material for no compensation or to checkmate you. For each diagram question, you may always use your discretion to award yourself 100 points for your chosen move unless there are clear instructions to the contrary.

As you play through the game use a sheet of paper to cover the page so that the test move under each diagram is not prematurely revealed.

1	d4	d6
2	♘f3	♘f6
3	c4	g6
4	♘c3	♗g7
5	e4	0-0
6	♗e2	e5
7	♗e3	

The Gligoric system, a perfectly viable alternative to the normal 7 ... 0-0. One virtue of the bishop move which has hitherto not been exploited is the fact that White may later choose to castle on the queenside

| | 7 | ... | exd4 |

Exchanging in the centre in this fashion indicates that Black plans to open up a bombardment against White's e-pawn. Viable alternatives which maintain the central tension are 7 ... ♘bd7, 7 ... ♕e7 and 7 ... h6, the last of which would meet 8 dxe5 with 8 ... ♘g4.

| | 8 | ♘xd4 | ♖e8 |
| | 9 | ♕c2 | |

9 f3 c6 10 ♕d2 d5 11 exd5 cxd5 12 0-0 ♘c6 13 c5 ♖xe3!? 14 ♕xe3 ♕f8! is an interesting exchange sacrifice that led to a draw in Karpov - Kasparov, World Championship Match (11), New York 1990.

| | 9 | ... | ♕e7 |
| | 10 | f3 | c6 |

Now examine the diagram and try to guess White's next move. Follow the same procedure throughout the rest of the game.

| | 11 | g4 |

250 points. A most extraordinary and courageous concept. I find it amazing that White can lash out in this fashion when the centre is still volatile and Black has possibilities such as ... d5 in reserve. It is especially impressive that such a young player as Kamsky should proceed with such overwhelming self-confidence against so experienced a champion as Tal. One point of White's 11th move is to attack fiercely by advancing the g- and h-pawns, another is to prevent 11 ... d5 which would be met by 12 g5 ♘h5 13 cxd5, winning a pawn for no compensation. Black now has a plethora of alternatives (11 ... h5, 11 ... ♘bd7, 11 ... ♘a6 etc). I suspect that Black's 11th move in the game is, in fact, much too slow and from this point on White seizes the initiative and maintains it vigorously until the end of the game.

| 11 | ... | a6 |
| 12 | g5 | ♘fd7 |

Before reading this note weigh the merits of Black alternatives, since a bonus is looming.

The natural move is 12 ... ♘h5 but then Tal must have feared 13 0-0-0 to be followed by f4 and ♗xh5, wrecking Black's kingside pawn constellation. It should be noted though that after 12 ... ♘h5 the immediate 13 f4 would fail both to 13 ... ♗xd4 or 13 ... ♘xf4 at once. However, after Black's 12th move in the game Tal's queenside forces remain congested and dormant while White's kingside offensive can proceed apace. Give yourself up to *100 bonus points* depending on how many of these ideas you saw.

What is White's next move?

13 h4

200 points. Thematically preparing to open the h-file.

13 ... b5

Black immediately commences the counter-attack. As White has already advanced his kingside pawns, Black is anticipating the queenside as the potential destination for the white king and thus hastens to open lines in that sector.

14 h5 b4

What is White's correct attacking procedure? Think hard, since a substantial bonus is in the offing.

15   hxg6

300 points. Kamsky's energetic handling of the assault against the black king reminds me forcibly of the savagery with which the youthful Tal himself used to conduct his attacks in the 1950's. If Black should accept the sacrifice with 15 ... bxc3 then 16 ♘f5 ♛f8 17 ♖xh7 would win, as indeed would 16 ... ♛e5 17 gxf7+ ♚xf7 18 ♖xh7 cxb2 19 ♖d1 ♖g8 20 ♗d4. Tal almost certainly did not bother to calculate any of these variations to their logical conclusion, he simply appreciated that in such situations the white knight cannot be permitted to penetrate to the f5-square. Award yourself up to *200 bonus points* depending on how much of this you saw.

15	...	hxg6
16	♘a4	d5

At last Black achieves the traditional breakthrough in the centre, which is meant to counter-act White's flank operations.

White's best now is?

17   0-0-0

150 points. The fruit of White's 7th move. If Black now plays 17 ... dxe4 White replies 18 f4, keeping the black knight out of e5, and then proceeds to double his rooks on the h-file. Instead, Tal decides to fight back by creating a passed pawn on the d-file. Award yourself *50 bonus points* if you saw the variation in this note.

17	...	c5
18	♘b3	d4
19	♗f4	♘c6

How does White prosecute his attack?

20 ♖h4

150 points. White's natural attacking plan is to double his rooks in the open h-file against the black king.

20	...	♘ce5
21	♖dh1	d3

Black must undertake something against the brutal threat of ♗d1 followed by ♕h2 and ♖h8+. The the text is designed to disrupt White's attacking formation.

22 ♗xd3 ♘xf3

Think deeply about the next move. A bonus is coming.

23 ♜h7

200 points. The critical moment of the game. It is here that Tal probably goes wrong, encouraging a trade of White's two rooks for the black queen which leads inexorably to White's advantage. The most combative move at this moment is the sacrificial 23 ... ♞de5, meeting 24 ♞axc5 with 24 ... ♝g4. Black's loss of a pawn is scarcely relevant. He can follow with ... ♜ac8 opening fire against the white king and also ... ♝h5 to staunch the h-file. After 23 ... ♞de5 24 ♞b6, White threatens both ♞xa8 and ♞d5. In that case Black should proceed with 24 ... ♝e6 25 ♞xa8 ♜xa8 with distinct compensation for the loss of the exchange. It should be noted that after 23 ♜h7 Black cannot play 23 ... ♞xg5 on account of 24 ♛h2 ♞xh7 25 ♛xh7+ ♚f8 26 ♝h6 when Black has no sensible defence. Up to *200 bonus points* depending on how much of this you saw.

23 ...   ♝e5
24 ♝xe5   ♛xe5

This appears to be another mistake, underestimating White's 25th move. There is a bonus coming now for finding Black's most effective defence. It would have been better to play 24 ... ♛xg5+ 25 ♚b1 and only now 25 ... ♛xe5. Perhaps after 24 ... ♛xg5+ Tal feared the remarkable response 25 ♛d2 meeting 25 ... ♞xd2 with 26 ♜h8 mate. Nevertheless after 25 ♛d2 ♜xe5 is an adequate defence. Award yourself *175 bonus points* if you appreciated that all this amounted to Black's best chance.

25 ♛g2   ♞d4

If instead 25 ... ♛xg5+ 26 ♛xg5 ♞xg5 27 ♜h8+ wins. White's next move is?

26 ♜h8+

150 points. This exchange gives White a winning endgame since Black cannot defend his pawns.

26	...	♕xh8
27	♖xh8+	♔xh8
28	♘bxc5	♘xc5
29	♘xc5	♘e6
30	♘a4	♗b7
31	♘b6	♖ad8

31 ... ♘c5 32 ♗c2 makes no difference.
White's next move is?

32 ♘d5

125 points. White must block the action of the black rooks in the centre.

32	...	♔g7

And here?

33 ♕f2

125 points. Much the best way of activating the white queen which can now penetrate the black camp via the dark squares on both the kingside and the queenside. White does not really have a material advantage, his prospects lie in the better mobility of his knight and queen.

33	...	♗xd5
34	♕f6+	♔g8
35	cxd5	♘c5
36	♔d2	a5
37	♕d4	♘d7
38	♗b5	♖f8
39	e5	♘b8
40	d6	♘d7
41	♔d3	♖fe8

Tal must have been in a dreadful time scramble, as his moves make a disjointed impression. He is, in any case, utterly lost but it is important to find White's accurate 42nd move. What is it?

42 ♗xd7

125 points. The last critical move of the game.

42	...	♖xd7
43	♔e4	♖dd8
44	♔d5	♖b8
45	d7	1-0

You should keep a record of your points scored on the table below so that you can add them up at the end of this book and calculate your exact chess strength.

Your points for this game. Tick one of these:

2500 ☐		1600+ ☐
2400+ ☐		1400+ ☐
2300+ ☐		1200+ ☐
2200+ ☐		1000+ ☐
2000+ ☐	less than 1000 ☐
1800+ ☐	

Kosten - Chandler
Hastings Premier 1990/91
Sicilian Defence

Your Target: 2600 points

Your partner is English grandmaster Murray Chandler. You have the black pieces and your opponent is Tony Kosten, who had recently earned the grandmaster title when this game was played.

You will be posed a series of questions during this game each of which is announced by a diagram. Points will be awarded for the correct answer and there will also be bonus points available for seeing correctly into difficult variations. The maximum amount of points available for this game is 2600, equivalent to a world championship candidate. At each diagram where a question is posed (but not in the bonus variations) you may use your own discretion to award yourself 100 points if you do not find the move played but choose instead any other move that does not allow your opponent to capture material for no compensation or to checkmate you. For each diagram question, you may always use your discretion to award yourself 100 points for your chosen move unless there are clear instructions to the contrary.

As you play through the game use a sheet of paper to cover the page so that the test move under each diagram is not prematurely revealed.

1	e4	c5
2	♘f3	e6
3	d4	cxd4
4	♘xd4	♘f6
5	♘c3	♘c6
6	♘db5	

Entering a full blooded Sveshnikov Sicilian, one of the most dangerous propositions for White. A safer way of playing for a small edge is 6 ♘xc6 bxc6 7 e5 ♘d5 8 ♘e4.

	6	...	**d6**
	7	**♗f4**	

Now examine the diagram and try to guess Black's next move. Follow the same procedure throughout the rest of the game.

	7	...	**e5**

150 points. Black is perfectly happy to accept the weakness on d5 in exchange for the dynamic counterplay he can generate by hounding White's minor pieces. In any case 7 ... ♘e5? fails to 8 ♕d4! with the nasty threat of ♘xd6+. Deduct *100 points* if you chose 7 ... ♘e5, or indeed any move other than 7 ... e5.

	8	**♗g5**	**a6**
	9	**♘a3**	**b5**
	10	**♗xf6**	**gxf6**
	11	**♘d5**	

Now, what did Black play?

	11	...	**♗g7**

200 points. A relatively modern way of handling this

variation for Black, the intention being to castle as quickly as possible and only then to seek to mobilise the mass
of central pawns. The formerly fashionable 11 ... f5 allows
White two double-edged piece sacrifices, 12 ♘xb5 axb5 13
♗xb5 ♕d7 14 exf5 or 12 ♗xb5 axb5 13 ♘xb5. In any case, if
you chose 11 ... f5, give yourself *150 points.*

12 ♗d3

What should Black play to challenge White's knight on
d5?

12 ... ♘e7

150 points. Relatively uncommon with 12 ... ♗e6 (also
150 points) being more usual. Nevertheless, it is extremely logical to challenge White's outpost knight in this fashion with the idea of retaining the bishop pair for later
use in the middlegame.

13	♘xe7	♕xe7
14	0-0	0-0
15	c4	

Before proceeding, think about the strategic ideas here,
since there is a bonus in the air.

Black is now strategically lost since if 15 ... bxc4 16
♘xc4 followed by ♘e3 emphasises Black's two key weaknesses, f5 and d5. Alternatively 15 ... b4 16 ♘c2 ♖b8 17
♘e3 leads to a similar outcome. Black has nothing for it
but to sacrifice his b5-pawn and therein lies his tactical
salvation. Although, by classical precepts, White has won
the strategic battle, the latent energy in the black position can survive the sacrifice of the entire queen's wing.
Award yourself up to *150 bonus points* depending on how
much of this variation you had foreseen, both in terms of
ideas, and variations.

What, in fact, did Black now play?

15   ...   f5!

200 points. If now 16 exf5 e4 threatening ... ♗xb2 and ... ♗xf5.

16   ♖e1   fxe4
17   ♗xe4   ♖b8
18   cxb5   axb5
19   ♕d3

A bonus is coming!

If now 19 ... b4 20 ♘c4 with many threats including ♗xh7+, ♕xd6 and ♘e3. The supine 19 ... ♗d7 allows 20 ♗xh7+ followed by 21 ♘f5. Also *150 bonus points* depending on how much of this you saw in advance.

So how did Black handle the threat to his pawns on b5 and h7?

19   ...   f5!

300 points. Black's hand is forced, the second thrust of his f-pawn is the only way to justify his play.

20   ♗d5+   ♔h8
21   ♘xb5   e4

22 ♕b3   ♗e5

Black's game now hangs on whether he can develop sufficient threats against White's kingside. On e5 Black's dark-squared bishop is an absolute tower of strength which cannot be opposed by any of the white minor pieces.

23 a4

It makes little difference as to move order. 23 ♖ac1 ♗d7 24 a4 transposes to the game. White should, however, avoid 24 ♗c6? ♗xc6 25 ♖xc6 when the sneaky 25 ... ♕b7 wins a piece.

23 ...   ♗d7
24 ♖ac1

What is Black's best in this volatile situation?

24 ...   ♕e8!

300 points. Hitting White on both flanks, threatening ... ♗xb5 and the transfer of the attack to the h-file by means of ... ♕h5 and perhaps ... ♖f6 - h6. After the game Chandler felt that White should now try 25 ♖c7. *150 bonus points* if you appreciated this.

25 ♗c4   ♕h5

The queen assumes its intended attacking position.

26 h3

This choice of defence evidently weakens White's resistance in the g-file but 26 g3 ♖f6 followed by ... ♖h6 would force White to make more concessions in his pawn front with h4. In any case, White had to try 26 g3, and hope to survive.

26 ...   ♕g6
27 ♗d5

How should Black continue his attack?

27 ...   ♖g8!

300 points. A brilliant sacrifice of the exchange meeting 28 ♗xg8 with 28 ... ♖xg8 29 g3 f4 threatening the devastating ... e3.

28 g3   ♖g7
29 ♖c7   ♕h5
30 ♖ec1

White cannot defend his h3-pawn.

30 ...   ♕xh3
31 ♖1c3

What is Black's next move?

31 ...   f4!

200 points. The most ruthless method of conducting the attack to a victorious finish. 31 ... ♖g6 32 ♖xd7 ♖h6 also looks devastating but after 31 ... ♖g6 White can muddy the waters with 32 ♘xd6 ♖xb3 33 ♘f7+ ♔g7 34 ♖xd7 but then 34 ... ♖xg3+ 35 ♖xg3 ♖xg3+ 36 fxg3 ♗d4 is terminal. However, 34 ♘xe5 is less clear. *150 bonus points* depending on how much of these variations was foreseen.

	32	▦xd7	fxg3
	33	▦f7	

How does Black finish off in style?

	33	...	♛h1+!

200 points. A fitting conclusion to a superb game.

	34	♔xh1	g2+
	35	♔g1	♞h2+

0-1

36 ♔xh2 g1(♛)+ 37 ♔h3 ♛h1 is checkmate.

You should keep a record of your points scored on the table below so that you can add them up at the end of this book and calculate your exact chess strength.

Your points for this game.
Tick one of these:

2600 ☐	1800+ ☐
2500+ ☐	1600+ ☐
2400+ ☐	1400+ ☐
2300+ ☐	1200+ ☐
2200+ ☐	1000+ ☐
2000+ ☐	less than 1000 ☐

6 Chandler - H. Olafsson
Hastings Premier 1990/91
Ruy Lopez

Your Target: 2600 points

Your partner is once again English grandmaster and Olympic team member Murray Chandler. You have the white pieces and your opponent is the top Icelandic grandmaster, Helgi Olafsson.

You will be posed a series of questions during this game each of which is announced by a diagram. Points will be awarded for the correct answer and there will also be bonus points available for seeing correctly into difficult variations. The maximum amount of points available for this game is 2600, equivalent to a world championship candidate. At each diagram where a question is posed (but not in the bonus variations) you may use your own discretion to award yourself 100 points if you do not find the move played but choose instead any other move that does not allow your opponent to capture material for no compensation or to checkmate you. For each diagram question, you may always use your discretion to award yourself 100 points for your chosen move unless there are clear instructions to the contrary.

As you play through the game use a sheet of paper to cover the page so that the test move under each diagram is not prematurely revealed.

1	e4	e5
2	♘f3	♘c6
3	♗b5	a6
4	♗a4	♘f6
5	0-0	♗e7
6	♕e2	

Chandler's pre-game analytical sweep of the records had indicated that Olafsson almost never defended the

Ruy Lopez. Murray therefore decided to choose the lesser known Worrall Variation which he felt would pose a non-Lopez player unusual problems. It is a perfectly respectable line, one point being that the white queen defends the e4-pawn, while White's king's rook can go in one move to d1, to offer support to the space-gaining thrust d4.

6	...	b5
7	♗b3	0-0
8	c3	d6
9	d4	♗g4

Now examine the diagram and try to guess White's next move. Follow the same procedure throughout the game.

10 ♖d1

150 points. The best way to support White's centre. As the perceptive reader will have observed, I gave a huge clue to this in my notes to 6 ♕e2.

10	...	♕c8
11	a4	b4

What is White's next move?

                        12   a5

250 points. To fix Black's a6-pawn as a weakness, but now Black has the chance to liquidate almost all of the queenside. The question is, is this good or bad for him?

                12   ...   bxc3
                13   bxc3   ♖b8

Now, what did White play?

                        14   ♗c4

150 points. Otherwise the bishop is too exposed to Black's rook.

                14   ...   exd4
                15   cxd4   ♘xa5

This series of tactics is the point of Black's defensive manoeuvre.

                16   ♖xa5   ♖xb1

Should White regain his pawn at once or switch to a dirct attack?

                        17   e5

150 points. This is unpleasant for Black since his knight is now driven to a square where it jams the kingside.

17	...	dxe5
18	dxe5	♞e8
19	♖xa6	♖b6

Should Chandler trade rooks or not? Look out for bonuses over the next few moves.

20 ♖a4

200 points. White must not exchange rooks prematurely since both of his are needed for the coming attack.

20 ... c5

Black's idea is clear – to play ... ♞c7-e6-d4. With hindsight safer would have been 20 ... g6, with the idea of transferring the knight to g7, which has a similar intention but without exposing the 7th rank to a rook invasion. *150 bonus points* for foreseeing the ideas in this note.

21 h3 ♗h5

Award yourself *150 bonus points* if you had foreseen that 21 ... ♗e6 was Black's best defence here.

22 ♖a7 ♞c7

White's next is crucial, not only a high scorer, but with bonuses attached. What is it?

23   e6‼

300 points. A deadly breakthrough. Black has four ways to capture this pawn, three of which are clearly and immediately fatal. For example: i) 23 ... ♘xe6 24 ♖xe7 wins a piece; ii) 23 ... ♕xe6 24 ♗xe6 wins Black's queen; iii) 23 ... ♖xe6 24 ♗xe6 winning the exchange with worse to follow. The fourth, 23 ... fxe6 fails to 24 ♕e5 forking the knight on c7 and the bishop on h5. Up to *200 bonus points* depending on how much of these variations you saw. Since White's e-pawn is immune, Black is forced to allow it to survive and Chandler now uses his advanced pawn to brilliant effect as a bludgeon to beat Black to his knees.

	23	...	♗f6
	24	e7	♖e8

Another key move is coming. Can you find it?

25   ♖d8!

300 points. A sensational irruption into the black camp.

	25	...	♖xd8

One final difficult move to find, with a bonus acompanying it. What is it?

26 ♖xc7

250 points. The second sacrifice, which cannot be accepted on account of 26 ... ♛xc7 27 e8(♛)+ ♖xe8 28 ♛xe8 mate. *200 bonus points* for seeing this. The upshot is that White wins a piece for no compensation at all.

26 ...　　　　♛b8

How does White finish off?

27 exd8(♛)+

150 points. A celebratory gift for an easy move to round off this wonderful game.

	27 ...	♛xd8
28	♗f4	g5
29	♗g3	♖b2
30	♛d3	♛a8
31	♛d7	♛a1+
32	♔h2	♖b1
33	♗xf7+	♔h8
34	♛e8+	♔g7
35	♗g6+	1–0

You should keep a record of your points scored on the table below so that you can add them up at the end of this book and calculate your exact chess strength.

　　Your points for this game. Tick one of these:

2600 ☐	1800+ ☐
2500+ ☐	1600+ ☐
2400+ ☐	1400+ ☐
2300+ ☐	1200+ ☐
2200+ ☐	1000+ ☐
2000+ ☐	less than 1000 ☐

Speelman - Sax
Hastings Premier 1990/91
English Opening

Your Target: 2600 points

Your partner is British grandmaster and world championship semi-finalist, Jonathan Speelman. You have the
white pieces and your opponent is the Hungarian grandmaster Gyula Sax.

You will be posed a series of questions during this
game each of which is announced by a diagram. Points will
be awarded for the correct answer and there will also be
bonus points available for seeing correctly into difficult
variations. The maximum amount of points available for
this game is 2600, equivalent to a world championship
candidate. **This game is so sharp and there are so many
"only moves" played that there is no dispensation on this
occasion to receive 100 points for moves that are not
mentioned.**

As you play through the game use a sheet of paper to
cover the page so that the test move under each diagram
is not prematurely revealed.

1   ♘f3

A restrained opening move, unlike the overt aggression
of 1 e4 or 1 d4. But that does not mean, in the hands of a
berserker like Speelman, that the middlegame will not
become fascinating.

1	...	♘f6
2	c4	c5
3	♘c3	♘c6
4	d4	cxd4
5	♘xd4	♛b6
6	♘b3	e6
7	a3	

Speelman's speciality. This edge pawn move looks

harmless, but has real teeth.

	7	...	d5

Gains free play for his pieces whilst simultaneously accepting the liability of an isolated pawn in the centre.

	8	♗e3	♛d8
	9	cxd5	♞xd5
	10	♞xd5	exd5
	11	g3	

Fianchettoing the king's bishop is the standard way to attack an isolated d-pawn.

	11	...	♗e7
	12	♗g2	♗f6

White now has to defend his b-pawn and I offer you the clue that the stereotyped 13 ♞d4, routinely occupying the square in front of Black's isolated d-pawn, would not yield very much. In that case White releases the pressure from the d5-pawn and Black, after castling, can consider ... ♞e5 - c4.

Now examine the diagram and try to guess White's next move. Follow the same procedure throughout the game.

	13	♛d2

200 points. Defending b2 and preparing to pile up on Black's d-pawn.

	13	...	d4!?

If 13 ... 0-0 14 ♖d1 and White is a little better. So Sax forces the action before White can get co-ordinated.

	14	♗xc6+	bxc6
	15	♗xd4	♛d5

Forking the knight on b3 and the rook on h1.

What did White play now? Two bonuses are coming up, as well, before the next diagram.

16   0-0-0!

300 points. Obviously White had to foresee this before his 13th move. In fact it is forced as otherwise White loses a piece, e.g. 16 ♕e3+ ♗e6! *150 bonus points* for seeing this.

16   ...   ♗g5!

If 16 ... ♕xb3? 17 ♗xf6 0-0 18 ♕g5 ♕c4+ 19 ♔d2 and White is winning as 19 ... ♕d5+ is forced, after which White is a pawn up with the better structure. *150 bonus points* for seeing this.

17   f4!   ♕xb3!

What should White play?

18   ♗xg7!?

200 points. A very risky move, very much in Speelman's style. If instead 18 fxg5 0-0 and now 19 ♕c3 forces a better ending, or alternatively White can keep the queens on with an unclear position, e.g. 19 ♖hf1 ♗g4 20 ♖f4 ♗h5. In view of this, also award yourself *200 points* if you chose 18 fxg5.

18   ...   ♗e7!

19   ♗xh8   f6!
20   e4

White is the exchange and two pawns up but his bishop on h8 is trapped and Black can quickly generate threats against the white king. White will always be able to give up his bishop for one more pawn and should be able to reach a reasonable ending, but it is not at all clear whether he can do any better.

Watch out for bonus points on the next move.

20   ...   ♔f7

The choice here was between the text and 20 ... ♖b8, but not 20 ... ♗g4? 21 e5 and White's bishop emerges in time. A possible continuation is 21 ... ♗xa3 22 ♗xf6 and after 22 ... ♗f5 or 22 ... ♖b8 23 e6! and the white bishop defends just in time. *150 bonus points* for seeing this.

We are now entering the critical phase of the game. The moves of both sides over the next few moves will decide the outcome, so stay continually alert for bonus points! First, though, what should White do here?

21   f5!?

300 points. Stopping the black queen's bishop from entering play on its best diagonal, c8-h3. Inferior to the text would be the immediate panicky attempt to rescue the stranded bishop: 21 e5? ♗f5 22 ♗xf6 ♗xa3 for if 23 e6+ ♔xf6 and Black wins. No points if you chose 21 e5? Speelman did, however, consider 21 ♕c2 ♕xc2+ 22 ♔xc2 ♗g4 23 ♗xf6! ♗xf6 when White is still doing well. Therefore give yourself *200 points* if you chose 21 ♕c2.

It should be observed that, paradoxical though it may seem, Black does not want to play 23 ... ♗xd1+ 24 ♖xd1 ♗xf6 - he does better to refrain from taking the exchange in order to use the bishops for blockading White's pawns.

21 ...   ♖b8

21 ... ♔g8 22 ♕d3 (not the pseudo-mating excursion 22 ♕h6?? ♗xh8 23 ♖d8+ ♗xd8 24 ♕f8+ ♕g8) and if 22 ... ♕xd3 23 ♖xd3 ♔xh8 24 ♖hd1 ♗g7 25 ♖d8! is strong for White adhering to the previous concept that White makes most progress by giving up one of his rooks for a valuable defensive bishop. Up to *200 bonus points* depending on how much of this you saw.

22 ♖he1   ♗a6??

This looks natural but is, in fact, a bad mistake in time trouble. Sax underestimates the importance of allowing a white rook to penetrate to d7 free of charge. However, Black cannot save himself with 22 ... ♗xa3? 23 ♗xf6! ♔xf6 24 ♕h6+ when White wins.

Also futile is 22 ... ♖b5 23 ♖e3 ♕a2 24 ♕c2 ♗f8 25 ♗xf6 ♗h6 26 ♖e1 ♕a1+ 27 ♔d2 ♗xe3+ 28 ♔e2 again winning easily.

22 ... ♔g8! is the best defence, when the position remains unclear. Up to *150 bonus points* depending on how many of these variations you saw in advance.

White's next is tricky. What is it? Also, more bonuses are in the pipeline for seeing deeply into the coming tactical ideas!

23 ♕c2

200 points. The time has come to trade into an endgame, which Black can scarcely avoid.

23 ...   ♕xc2+

If 23 ... ♕a2 24 e5 ♖xb2 25 e6+ ♔f8 26 ♕xb2 ♗xa3 27 ♖d8+ ♔e7 28 ♗xf6 checkmate is an attractive finish. *150 bonus points* for seeing this.

24	♔xc2	♖xh8

With 23 ... ♗a6 Black has effectively lost two tempi enabling White to invade with the rooks. If Black decides to retract his previous idea and defend d7 with 24 ... ♗c8 then 25 g4 ♔g8 26 ♗xf6 ♗xf6 27 e5 wins. *150 bonus points* depending on how much of this you saw.

25	♖d7	♖d8
26	♖xa7	♗d3+
27	♔c3	♔f8?

Losing at once. Think carefully now about possible alternative Black defences. A bonus is coming for this. The only move was 27 ... c5 28 b3 ♔f8 and now White should probably play 29 ♖d1 ♗xe4 30 ♖xd8+ ♗xd8 31 ♖xh7 which should win. Not, however, 30 ♖xe7 ♔xe7 31 ♖e1 and now Black has 31 ... ♖d4 defending the bishop. Award yourself up to *150 bonus points* depending on how much of this was foreseen. How does White now finish off?

28	♖d1

150 points. This, in conjunction with White's next, wins.

28	...	♗xe4

29 ♖xe7

This move is now necessary, but it forces resignation. No other move makes any sense at all, so if you did not choose 29 ♖xe7 deduct *300 points*. After 29 ... ♔xe7 30 ♖e1, the previous ... ♖d4 resource is no longer available. Thus White emerges two pawns ahead with a trivial win.

1–0

I would like to thank Jon Speelman for demonstrating variations from this fascinating game to me.

You should keep a record of your points scored on the table below so that you can add them up at the end of this book and calculate your exact chess strength.

Your points for this game.
Tick one of these:

2600 ☐	1800+ ☐
2500+ ☐	1600+ ☐
2400+ ☐	1400+ ☐
2300+ ☐	1200+ ☐
2200+ ☐	1000+ ☐
2000+ ☐	less than 1000 ☐

8

Larsen - Wolff
London 1990
Pirc Defence

Your Target: 2600 points

Your partner is Danish grandmaster and three times world championship semi-finalist, Bent Larsen. You have the white pieces and your opponent is Patrick Wolff, the young American grandmaster.

You will be posed a series of questions during this game each of which is announced by a diagram. Points will be awarded for the correct answer and there will also be bonus points available for seeing correctly into difficult variations. The maximum amount of points available for this game is 2600, equivalent to a world championship candidate. At each diagram where a question is posed (but not in the bonus variations) you may use your own discretion to award yourself 100 points if you do not find the move played but choose instead any other move that does not allow your opponent to capture material for no compensation or to checkmate you. For each diagram question, you may always use your discretion to award yourself 100 points for your chosen move unless there are clear instructions to the contrary.

As you play through the game use a sheet of paper to cover the page so that the test move under each diagram is not prematurely revealed.

1	♘f3	g6
2	e4	♗g7
3	d4	d6
4	h3	♘f6
5	♘c3	0-0
6	♗e3	d5
7	e5	♘e4
8	♗d3	

58 *Larsen - Wolff*

Larsen sidesteps the critical variation of this unusual opening which involves pawn sacrifices for Black that would occur after 8 ♘xe4 dxe4 9 ♘g5 c5. This was probably a sensible decision against Wolff who is one of the most booked-up players on the contemporary tournament circuit. The closed position which now develops, although satisfactory for Black, will be much less to Wolff's taste.

| | 8 | ... | ♘xc3 |
| | 9 | bxc3 |

White has now contracted doubled pawns. However, these are not just a source of weakness, they also help to buttress White's centre. You must utilise this factor in the coming play.

9	...	c5
10	0-0	♘c6
11	♕d2	♕a5
12	♖fb1	a6
13	a4	♖b8

Now examine the diagram and try to guess White's next move. Follow the same procedure throughout the rest of the game.

14 ♕c1

300 points. This move sets a cunning trap and prepares to bombard Black's queenside via the b-file.

14 ... ♗e6

Of course not 14 ... ♕xc3 15 ♗d2 trapping Black's queen. *200 bonus points* for seeing this in advance.

15	♕b2	c4
16	♗e2	♕c7
17	♕b6	♕d7
18	♗f4	h6

19   a5   g5

This thrust looks aggressive, but Black is also weakening himself. You should now be thinking of ways to take advantage of this.

20   ♘g3   ♗f5

Now, what did White play?

21   ♕b2

300 points. This seemingly paradoxical retreat defends c2 and prepares to swing the queen over to attack Black's kingside. After 21 e6 ♕xe6 22 ♗xb8 ♕xe2 White's position is liable to fall apart. The doubled pawns would then become very weak. No points for this idea.

21   ...   ♘a7

What is White's next move?

22   ♕c1

300 points. This move is necessary before ... ♘b5 nails White's queen to the spot on b2 by forcing it to defend the c3-pawn. Again 22 e6 ♕xe6 23 ♗xb8 and now 23 ... ♖xb8 gives Black too much compensation for the sacrificed exchange. Nothing for this, or indeed for any other white choice on move 22.

22 ...   ♘b5

This is an excellent square for the knight. It cannot be driven away and blocks the b-file.

23 ♕d2   ♖bc8
24 ♖e1   f6
25 ♗f1   ♗e4
26 ♘h2

Black's next move is a mistake. You should be thinking very carefully here about what Black's best defence is on move 26.

26 ...   f5

A blunder which allows White to take control. There is a huge bonus coming for Black's correct move, so think carefully about it before proceeding.

Correct would have been 26 ... fxe5 27 ♗xe5 ♗xe5 28 dxe5 when Black's superior central structure is counterbalanced by the evidently shaky nature of his kingside pawns. If in this variation White reacts to 26 ... fxe5 with 27 f3 hoping for 27 ... ♗g6 28 ♗xe5 ♗xe5 29 ♖xe5 with obvious domination, Black can instead turn the tables by means of the sacrifice 27 ... exd4 28 fxe4 ♘xc3 29 exd5 ♕xd5 30 ♖xe7 ♘e4 31 ♕e1 d3 with fierce counterplay. Award yourself up to *400 bonus points* depending on how much of all this you saw.

Now, how did White proceed?

27 f3

200 points. The refutation of Black's play.

27 ...   f4

Should White move his threatened bishop – if so, to where?

28 ♗xf4

200 points. Wolff had overlooked this desperado capture thinking that White's choices were restricted either to 28 ♗f2 or 28 fxe4 fxg3, both of which would be fine for Black.

	28	...	♖xf4
	29	fxe4	dxe4
	30	♕e3	♕c6

Now, what did White play?

31 g3

200 points. To drive away the black rook. Black's position is now falling apart and he must sacrifice material in order to stay in the game. In particular, Black's major problem is the massive wedge of white central pawns standing in the path of his king's bishop.

| | 31 | ... | ♖f3 |

Any other move by Black is refuted by 32 ♗g2, followed by ♗xe4.

	32	♘xf3	exf3
	33	♔f2	♘c7

34 ♕e4   ♘d5

White now needs to contain Black's counter-attack. How does he do it? Also, a bonus is in the air.

35 ♖e3

200 points. An extraordinary move. After 35 ... ♘xe3 36 ♕xc6 ♖xc6 37 ♔xe3 Black loses since he cannot defend his weak pawns on b7, c4 and f3. Furthermore his bishop on g7 is quite locked out of the game. *150 bonus points* if you saw this.

35 ...   g4

An ingenious try since if now 36 hxg4 ♘xe3 37 ♕xc6 Black has the interposition 37 ... ♘xg4+.

36 ♖b1   h5
37 hxg4   ♘xe3
38 ♕xe3   hxg4

One final strong move is required to break down Black's resistance. What is it?

39 ♖b6

150 points. The complications have resulted in Larsen giving back his extra material but now he turns his atten-

tion to Black's debilitated king's flank, which can no
longer be protected.

| | 39 ... | ♛a4 |

Or 39 ... ♛d5 40 ♛g5 with the threat of ♖g6.

| | 40 ♛e4 | ♛xa5 |
| | 41 ♖g6 | 1-0 |

There is no sensible defence to ♛xg4.

You should keep a record of your points scored on the
table below so that you can add them up at the end of
this book and calculate your exact chess strength.

> Your points for this game.
> Tick one of these:

2600 ☐	1800+ ☐
2500+ ☐	1600+ ☐
2400+ ☐	1400+ ☐
2300+ ☐	1200+ ☐
2200+ ☐	1000+ ☐
2000+ ☐	less than 1000 ☐

9

King - Larsen
London 1990
Ruy Lopez

Your Target: 2600 points

Your partner is once again Danish grandmaster Bent Larsen, three times a world championship semi-finalist. You have the black pieces and your opponent is Daniel King, one of England's leading grandmasters.

    You will be posed a series of questions during this game each of which is announced by a diagram. Points will be awarded for the correct answer and there will also be bonus points available for seeing correctly into difficult variations. The maximum amount of points available for this game is 2600, equivalent to a world championship candidate. At each diagram where a question is posed (but not in the bonus variations) you may use your own discretion to award yourself 100 points if you do not find the move played but choose instead any other move that does not allow your opponent to capture material for no compensation or to checkmate you. For each diagram question, you may always use your discretion to award yourself 100 points for your chosen move unless there are clear instructions to the contrary.

    As you play through the game use a sheet of paper to cover the page so that the test move under each diagram is not prematurely revealed.

1	e4	e5
2	♘f3	♘c6
3	♗b5	a6
4	♗a4	♘f6
5	0–0	♗e7
6	♖e1	b5
7	♗b3	d6
8	c3	♘a5

9	♗c2	c5
10	d4	♛c7
11	a4	

Now examine the diagram and try to guess Black's next move. Follow the same procedure throughout the rest of the game.

| 11 | ... | c4 |

200 points. White's threat of 12 axb5 axb5 13 b4 can now be met by 13 ... cxb3. Also, White now has a weakness on b3 which Black might exploit in the further course of the game.

12	♘bd2	0–0
13	♘f1	♖e8
14	♗g5	h6
15	♗h4	♘h7
16	♗g3	

More prudent would be 16 ♗xe7 but White has a grandiose scheme in mind which will be revealed on his next move.

Now, how did Black proceed?

16 ...   ♘g5

150 points. Seeking to eliminate White's pressure against e5 in the most active fashion possible, for if now 17 dxe5 ♘xf3+ 18 ♕xf3 dxe5. A bonus is coming if you consider White's reply.

17 ♘xe5

The point of White's play. For his sacrificed piece he obtains two pawns and a dangerous attack. *150 bonus points* if you saw this idea in advance.

17 ...   dxe5

18 ♗xe5

Black's queen is attacked. How should the threat be parried?

18 ...   ♕b6

300 points. The best square for the black queen, from here it can switch to direct defence of the threatened black king's wing.

19 ♘e3   ♗b7

It is more important from Black's point of view to stop ♘d5 rather than ♘f5.

20 ♘f5   ♗f8
21 h4   ♘h7
22 ♕g4   ♕g6
23 ♕f4   ♘b3

Consider how White should reply now. There is a bonus coming up if you get it right.

24 ♖ad1

Natural enough but more trenchant might have been 24 ♗xb3 cxb3 25 ♖e3 with the idea of ♖g3. *200 bonus points* if you saw this idea in advance.

Now, how did Black proceed?

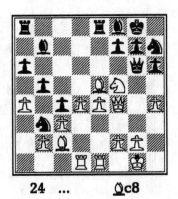

24 ...   ♗c8

200 points.

25 ♖e3

What should Black do about the terrible menace of 26 ♖g3?

25 ...   ♗xf5

200 points. Eliminating a dangerous aggressor.

26 exf5   ♛h5

This is the crisis of the game and there are huge bonuses coming up for White's possibilities here and Black's defences.

27 f6

At first sight this thrust appears murderous but in fact White has overlooked the availability of a vitally important defensive resource. Superior would have been 27 ♖de1 though 27 ... f6 holds up for Black. *200 bonus points* for seeing this.

What is Black's next move? There is a big reward for spotting the correct defence, including a large bonus for accurate calculation!

27 ...   ♘xf6

400 points. At this point it might appear that White can win outright with 28 ♗xf6 ♖xe3 (if 28 ... gxf6 White wins with 29 ♖g3+) 29 ♕xe3 gxf6 30 ♕e4 threatening checkmate and the black rook on a8. Nevertheless, at this point Larsen has a diabolical counter namely 30 ... ♕g6! when 31 ♕xa8 ♕xc2 hands over the initiative to Black. *300 bonus points* if you saw all of this before playing 27 ... ♘xf6. What White plays, probably demoralised by the resilience of Black's defence, is scarcely an improvement.

28 ♖de1   ♘d5
29 ♕e4

This looks crushing, threatening ♕xd5 and ♕h7 mate, but you have already been given a clue about Black's best defence, which is ... ?

29 ...   ♕g6

200 points. Once again, the key to Black's defence. 29 ... ♘f6 30 ♕f4 gets just *100 points*, the standard for playable alternatives.

30 ♕xg6

Now it is clear that if 30 ♕xd5 ♕xc2.

30	...	fxg6
31	♖g3	♘e7
32	♗e4	♖ad8

Bonus coming. Think hard about White's next move!

33	axb5

The last chance to maintain resistance would have been 33 ♗b7. *100 bonus points* if you saw this.

33	...	axb5
34	♖f1	♘d2
35	♖e1	♘xe4
36	♖xe4	♔h7
37	♖f3	♔g8
38	♖ef4	♘c6
39	♗c7	♖d7
	0-1	

You should keep a record of your points scored on the table below so that you can add them up at the end of this book and calculate your exact chess strength.

Your points for this game.
Tick one of these:

2600	☐	1800+	☐
2500+	☐	1600+	☐
2400+	☐	1400+	☐
2300+	☐	1200+	☐
2200+	☐	1000+	☐
2000+	☐	less than 1000	☐

10

Larsen - King
Hastings Premier 1990/91
Bogo-Indian Defence

Your Target: 2600 points

Yet again, your partner is Danish grandmaster Bent Larsen. You have the white pieces and your opponent is again the English grandmaster Daniel King.

You will be posed a series of questions during this game each of which is announced by a diagram. Points will be awarded for the correct answer and there will also be bonus points available for seeing correctly into difficult variations. The maximum amount of points available for this game is 2600, equivalent to a world championship candidate. At each diagram where a question is posed (but not in the bonus variations) you may use your own discretion to award yourself 100 points if you do not find the move played but choose instead any other move that does not allow your opponent to capture material for no compensation or to checkmate you. For each diagram question, you may always use your discretion to award yourself 100 points for your chosen move unless there are clear instructions to the contrary.

As you play through the game use a sheet of paper to cover the page so that the test move under each diagram is not prematurely revealed.

1	♘f3	♘f6
2	d4	e6
3	c4	♗b4+
4	♗d2	♕e7
5	g3	♘c6
6	♗g2	♗xd2+

Now examine the diagram and try to guess White's next move. Follow the same procedure throughout the rest of the game.

7 ♘bxd2

200 points. Rarely played in general. Conventional wisdom dictates that White should normally recapture with the queen on d2 and then place his queen's knight on the superior square c3. However, by capturing on d2 at the precise moment he has granted Black the resource 7 ♕xd2 ♘e4 8 ♕c2 ♕b4+ which is somewhat annoying. Therefore, White has little choice but to capture with the knight in this specific situation. Therefore 7 ♕xd2 gets no points.

7 ... d6

Extra protection for the central dark squares. Black is preparing to stake a claim with ... e5.

8 0-0

X-ray pressure from White's bishop on g2 against the black queen's flank means that White has emerged from the opening with a small edge. Think now about Black's strategy. There will be a bonus available.

8 ... a5

Interestingly, King defers the natural move 8 ... 0-0 since then 9 e4 e5 10 d5 ♘b8 11 b4 a5 12 a3 gives White a serious space advantage on the queenside. *150 bonus points* for appreciating this.

9 e4 e5
10 d5 ♘b8
11 ♘e1 h5

Not an every day sort of move. Black's idea, though, is not so much to attack White's king as to provoke 12 h4 and thus grant Black use of g4 for a minor piece should White ever advance himself with f4. 11 ... 0-0 is more stereotyped and gives White a simple plan of ♘d3 plus f4.

Now, how did White proceed?

12   h4

300 points. It is, in fact, absolutely necessary to stop the further onward march of Black's h-pawn. This is far more important than giving away the future occupation of the g4-square to either a black knight or a black bishop.

12   ...   0-0

The time has come to castle. Black's pawns on h5 looks like a weakness but it is no more of disadvantage than White's pawn on h4.

13   ♘d3   ♗d7
14   ♕e2   ♘a6

What is White's next move?

15   b3

150 points. Engaging Black on the queenside. It now appears that White is preparing to play a3, ♖ab1 and b4. Deduct *50 points* if you played 15 a3 allowing Black to play ... a4 when White's pawns could never advance.

15   ...   c6

Rapidly establishing potential counterplay in the c-file. How should White react to this?

16   ☐fc1

150 points. Fortunately for White, Black cannot now try 16 ... cxd5 17 cxd5 b5 since 18 a4 bxa4 19 bxa4 presents White with the annoying threat of ♘c4, when Black's queenside is weaker than White's.

16   ...   ☐fc8

Should White now continue on the queenside, and if so, by what means?

17   a4

150 points. Energetic measures are required to prevent the exchange on d5 plus ... b5, which Black's last move had prepared, but now White abandons any thought of advancing on the queenside and also surrenders his control of dark squares on the left flank. Now think carefully about Black's possible ideas. A bonus is coming.

17   ...   b6

Can this really be good? By liquidating the cohesion of his pawns on c6 and b7 King immediately presents White with use of the d5-square for future occupation. Either a waiting policy was called for such as 17 ... g6 or even sealing the queenside entirely with 17 ... c5. In that case White's only winning plan would be a long term f4–break which, as I stated before, would grant Black permanent use of g4 for his bishop or knight.

Nevertheless, King stoutly maintained that his decision on move 17 was correct. He wanted to rule out any tactical ideas by White involving c5, followed by ♘c4, and he wanted to give himself the possibility of playing ... ♘c5 and be able to recapture after ♘xc5 with his b6-pawn. Depending on how much of this you appreciated, give yourself *200 bonus points*.

What did White play now?

18 dxc6

150 points. This does not necessarily confer an advantage on White but it is the only move available if he wants to try for a win. Think about Black's recapture. There is a bonus coming here and on Black's 19th move as well.

18 ...   ♖xc6

White's strategy is now justified by this excessively passive recapture. Black must play 18 ... ♗xc6 followed by ... ♘c7 – e6 with a fully viable position. *200 bonus points* if you realised that Black had to recapture on c6 with the bishop.

19 ♘b1   g6

Under pressure from White's looming manoeuvre ♘c3 - d5 Black panics. Correct would be 19 ... ♗g4 20 ♗f3 ♗xf3 21 ♕xf3 ♘c5 22 ♘xc5 dxc5 and although Black's position is rather dormant, it is very difficult to breach. Up to *200 bonus points* depending on how much of this you saw.

20 ♘c3   ♕d8

How does Larsen now increase the pressure?

21 ♖a2

250 points. Slowly but surely bringing up his reserves. Larsen now has a number of trumps to play with: weak black pawns on b6 and d6, occupation of d5 with a minor piece and finally, the f4-break, now that Black has forfeited much of the resilience of his structure.

	21	...	♗g4
	22	♕e3	♕f8
	23	♖d2	♖b8
	24	f3	♗c8
	25	♖cd1	♘e8
	26	♘b5	

Evidently Larsen's prime task is to tie Black down to defence of d6 so that when f4 comes Black's king's knight will not be able to transfer easily to the molesting g4-square.

	26	...	♔h7

Is it time to attack? If so, how and where?

27 f4

250 points. Having tied Black down on the queenside

and in the centre the correct strategy in such situations is to break through by opening a second front. This second front is the f-file which can be swiftly be occupied by White's rooks. Given the dramatic events now in train the weakening of the g4-square entailed by 27 f4 is of no significance. Indeed, Black is never even given time to occupy this weakened square with one of his pieces.

| 27 | ... | ♕e7 |
| 28 | f5 | ♕f8 |

Suffering in silence, but 28 ... gxf5 29 exf5 opens up a deadly attack from g2 against the black rook on c6. What follows is dreadful as Larsen whips up sudden and fearful attack.

| 29 | ♖f1 | ♕h6 |
| 30 | fxg6+ | ♕xg6 |

How does White finish off?

| 31 | ♘a7 | |

250 points. The *coup de grâce.*

31	...	♖c7
32	♘xc8	♖cxc8
33	♗h3	

Threatening the rook and 34 ♗f5, netting Black's queen.

| 33 | ... | ♔g8 |
| 34 | ♗f5 | 1-0 |

Total carnage, Black loses the exchange, his b-pawn, and he also has no real defence to White doubling rooks in the f-file.

You should keep a record of your points scored on the table below so that you can add them up at the end of this book and calculate your exact chess strength.

Your points for this game.
Tick one of these:

2600 ☐		1800+ ☐
2500+ ☐		1600+ ☐
2400+ ☐		1400+ ☐
2300+ ☐		1200+ ☐
2200+ ☐		1000+ ☐
2000+ ☐	less than 1000 ☐	

11

Short - Seirawan
Manila Interzonal 1990
Caro-Kann Defence

Your Target: 2600 points

Your partner is England's leading grandmaster and world championship candidate Nigel Short. You have the white pieces and your opponent is Yasser Seirawan, a world championship candidate himself, and top-ranked grandmaster in the United States. This was a needle game for both players in their campaign to qualify for the world championship candidates competition from the Manila Interzonal tournament, so both sides were desperately seeking a win.

You will be posed a series of questions during this game each of which is announced by a diagram. Points will be awarded for the correct answer and there will also be bonus points available for seeing correctly into difficult variations. The maximum amount of points available for this game is 2600, equivalent to a world championship candidate. At each diagram where a question is posed (but not in the bonus variations) you may use your own discretion to award yourself 100 points if you do not find the move played but choose instead any other move that does not allow your opponent to capture material for no compensation or to checkmate you. For each diagram question, you may always use your discretion to award yourself 100 points for your chosen move unless there are clear instructions to the contrary.

As you play through the game use a sheet of paper to cover the page so that the test move under each diagram is not prematurely revealed.

1   e4   c6

The Caro-Kann Defence introduced with this move enjoys a reputaton for great solidity. It was first mentioned by the Italian writer on chess Giulio Cesare Polerio as early as 1590. The name, however stems from the analysis of the British player Horatio Caro and the Viennese master Marcus Kann in their magazine *Bruderschaft*, from 1886. Nevertheless, the Caro-Kann did not become fully respectable until it was adopted by Nimzowitsch and Capablanca, and it did not appear in a World Championship until Botvinnik used it in 1958. Nowadays, it is a favourite of Anatoly Karpov and of Jon Speelman.

	2	d4	d5
	3	e5	

The Advance Variation, the least explored of White's options. More common, but leading to a less tense struggle, is 3 ♘c3 dxe4 4 ♘xe4 when Black has a choice between 4 ... ♘d7, 4 ... ♘f6 or 4 ... ♗f5.

	3	...	♗f5
	4	c3	e6
	5	♗e2	c5

It is generally considered worth sacrificing the time involved in the double move of Black's c-pawn in order to unleash an offensive against White's central bastions.

	6	♘f3	♘c6
	7	0-0	h6

I find this move difficult to comprehend. Surely it is more consistent to increase the pressure against White's centre by means of 7 ... ♕b6?

	8	♗e3	cxd4

The American grandmaster must have been reluctant to relinquish the tension by this seemingly premature exchange, which grants White's queen's knight a superb square on c3, to invade the black queen's flank. Nevertheless, if Black continues with the seemingly more flexible 8 ... ♘ge7, then 9 dxc5 ♘g6 10 ♗b5 poses problems as to how Black can regain his pawn.

	9	cxd4	♘ge7
	10	♘c3	♘c8

A somewhat convoluted regrouping but Seirawan evidently did not wish to play ... ♘g6 since this would have cut off the retreat of his bishop on f5.

Now examine the diagram and try to guess White's next move. Follow the same procedure throughout the rest of the game.

11 ♖c1

300 points. It is very important to be the first to occupy the open c-file, the main jumping–off post for invading the black position. There will be a bonus for getting Black's reply right.

11 ... a6

This looks too slow. He should prefer the immediate 11 ... ♘b6. *100 bonus points* if you appreciated this. Now White's queen's knight enters play with tremendous effect.

12 ♘a4 ♘b6

White's next should not be too difficult. What is it?

13 ♘c5

200 points. The point of White's play. By occupying the outpost square c5 White accentuates his pressure in the c–file.

	13	...	♗xc5
	14	♖xc5	0-0
	15	♕b3	♘d7
	16	♖c3	♕b6

Work out White's next and think about alternatives, since a bonus is also attached to this move.

17 ♖fc1

300 points. Short has obviously won the battle of the opening but he must proceed with great care if he is to nurse his advantage to victory. Here, for example, it would be premature to play 17 ♕xb6 ♘xb6 18 ♖b3 ♘c4 19 ♖xb7 ♘6a5 with counterplay. Alternatively 17 ♕xb6 ♘xb6 18 ♖b3 ♘c4 19 ♗xc4 dxc4 20 ♖xb7 ♖ab8, again with substantial compensation for the lost pawn. Short's method, quietly tightening the noose, is clearly preferable. Up to *300 bonus points* depending on how much of this you saw.

	17	...	♕xb3
	18	♖xb3	♖fb8
	19	♘d2	

The second white knight moves into an attacking position.

| | 19 | ... | ♔f8 |

White's next move is very subtle. What is it?

20 h4

400 points. The hallmark of a great master. White's prospects appear to lie exclusively on the queenside, but Short now strengthens his hand by stealing some space on the opposite wing. In fact, it is the subtle combination of attacks on both sides of the board which ultimately decides the game in White's favour.

20	...	♔e8
21	g4	♗h7
22	h5	♘d8
23	♖bc3	♘b6
24	♘b3	♘a4

White's next is not too difficult. What is it?

25 ♖c7

200 points. Sacrificing a pawn in the interests of establishing a powerful rook on the seventh rank. Nothing for anything else in this case, for White's rook is under attack and it actually has no other safe square.

25	...	♘xb2
26	♘c5	b5

How does White prosecute his attack?

27 g5

300 points. The attack is reaching its climax with threats such as gxh6 or g6. Black's next move seeks to staunch White's pressure in the c-file, but in the meantime Short has found another and more deadly use for his rook on c1.

27 ...   ♘c4

Black's knight at last reaches the outpost for which it has been striving, but its triumph on this square is short-lived.

28 gxh6   gxh6
29 ♘d7   ♘xe3

This exchange at least eliminates the threat of ♗xh6, but now a fresh avenue is opened for the white attack.

30 fxe3   ♗f5

Black is normally happy to develop his bishop on f5 in the Caro-Kann but it is remarkable in this game how impotent this piece has been in spite of its almost complete freedom of action.

Should Short now take the black rook, or is there something stronger?

31 ♔f2

250 points for this and *150* for 31 ♘xb8. There is nothing wrong with taking the exchange but since Black is so trussed up Short has greater ambitions than simple win of material.

31 ...   ♖b7
32 ♘f6+

Weaving the mating net.

32 ...   ♔f8

Can you find White's next bone-crusher?

33 ♖g1!!   1–0

250 points for this and nothing for anything else. The *coup de grâce* which breaks Black's resistance and at the same time the most elegant conclusion to White's far-ranging offensive. After 33 ... ♖xc7 White forces checkmate with 34 ♖g8+ ♔e7 35 ♖e8 mate.

You should keep a record of your points scored on the table below so that you can add them up at the end of this book and calculate your exact chess strength.

Your points for this game.
Tick one of these:

2600	☐	1800+	☐
2500+	☐	1600+	☐
2400+	☐	1400+	☐
2300+	☐	1200+	☐
2200+	☐	1000+	☐
2000+	☐	less than 1000	☐

12

Short - Adams
James Capel Challenge 1988
Caro-Kann Defence

Your Target: 2600 points

Your partner is once again the top English grandmaster Nigel Short. You have the white pieces and your opponent is Michael Adams, the rising star of British chess.

You will be posed a series of questions during this game each of which is announced by a diagram. Points will be awarded for the correct answer and there will also be bonus points available for seeing correctly into difficult variations. The maximum amount of points available for this game is 2600, equivalent to a world championship candidate. At each diagram where a question is posed (but not in the bonus variations) you may use your own discretion to award yourself 100 points if you do not find the move played but choose instead any other move that does not allow your opponent to capture material for no compensation or to checkmate you. For each diagram question, you may always use your discretion to award yourself 100 points for your chosen move unless there are clear instructions to the contrary.

As you play through the game use a sheet of paper to cover the page so that the test move under each diagram is not prematurely revealed.

1	e4	c6
2	d4	d5
3	♘c3	dxe4
4	♘xe4	♘d7
5	♗c4	♘gf6
6	♘g5	e6
7	♕e2	♘b6
8	♗b3	h6

Black cannot play the tempting 8 ... ♕xd4 on account

of 9 ♘1f3 ♕d8 10 ♘e5 with a decisive attack on f7.

9	♘5f3	c5
10	c3	cxd4
11	♘xd4	♗e7
12	♘gf3	0-0
13	0-0	♗d7
14	♘e5	♗a4

Now examine the diagram and try to guess White's next move. Follow the same procedure throughout the rest of the game.

15 ♗f4

200 points. Due to the impressive mobilization of White's forces, Black is already skating on thin ice. Thus, Short could instead have tried 15 ♘xe6 fxe6 16 ♗xe6+ ♔h8 17 ♘g6+ ♔h7 18 ♘xe7 ♕xe7 19 ♗f5+ when Black is lost. Fortunately for Adams, though, Black has the superior 16 ... ♔h7 at his disposal, when White has no clear continuation of his attack. *200 bonus points* if you saw all of this.

15 ...   ♕c8

Does White have any tactics available here?

16	♘g6

250 points.

16	...	♖e8

Of course, 16 ... fxg6 would fail miserably to 17 ♗xe6+ winning Black's queen. *100 bonus points* if you saw this when you played 16 ♘g6.

17	♘xe7+	♖xe7
18	♘f5	♖d7
19	♗xa4	♘xa4

Now there is a difficult decision. Should White advance or retreat?

20	♘xg7

500 points. Advance! White has sacrificed a piece not only to shatter the black king's wing, but also to expose the black knight which has been lured to a4. White's next move, pinning the black knight on f6, makes both these motifs clear.

20	...	♔xg7
21	♗e5	♕c6
22	♕g4+	♔h7

Black has been unable to save his extra piece, indeed, he has now lost a pawn and his king's fortifications appear smashed. Most onlookers believed that Black was lost, but now the talented teenager from Truro whips up a ferocious counter-attack in the open g-file.

23	♗xf6	♖g8
24	♕h3	♘xb2
25	♗d4	♖g6
26	f4	f5
27	♖f3	♕e4
28	♖e3	♕xf4

In order to beat off Black's pressure, White has been obliged to jettison his f4-pawn.

29 ♖ae1 ♛d6

White is a pawn down and needs a good move. What is it?

30 ♖xe6

500 points. After the game Short pointed out that this sacrifice of the rook was the only way to keep his chances alive. No points for anything else.

30 ... ♖xe6
31 ♛xf5+ ♖g6
32 h4 ♖e7

Can White win back his rook? Think carefully before proceeding, since a bonus is available.

If now 33 ♖xe7+ ♛xe7 34 h5 then Black wins with 34 ... ♛e1+ 35 ♔h2 ♛g3+ 36 ♔h1 ♛xg2 mate. Award yourself 200 bonus points for seeing this. Short's next move is a brilliant resource which not only deflects Black's initiative, but also permits White's own offensive to flare up.

33 ♖e2!!

500 points. A wonderfully imaginative conception. White now threatens 34 h5 winning the pinned rook on g6, as well as 34 ♖xb2. Faced with such a coup Adams does well not to suffer instant nervous collapse.

33	...	♕d7

Not 33 ... ♖xe2 34 ♕f7+ ♖g7 35 ♕xg7 mate.

34	♕f8	♖eg7
35	♖xb2	♖g8
36	♕f3	b6
37	h5	♖g5
38	♖f2	♖e8

Sensibly seizing the important open file.

39	♕d3+	♔g8
40	♖f6	♖e6
41	♕c4	♖d5

What is White's next move?

42   ♖g6+

150 points. It is vital, given that White is the exchange down, to create a counter-balancing passed pawn.

42	...	♖xg6
43	hxg6	b5
44	♕b3	♕e6
45	♕b1	♖g5

Black should, perhaps, have tried 45 ... ♕e2.

46	g7	a6

If now 46 ... ♕e2 47 ♕b3+ ♔c4 48 ♕d1 averts Black's counter-attack against g2.

47	♕f1	♕e7
48	♕f2	♖xg7

Realistically, Black has no way of exploiting his advantage of rook against bishop given White's towering compensation in the form of the passed pawn on g7. Adams, therefore, liquidates to a drawn queen and pawn endgame.

> 49 ♗xg7 ♔xg7
> 50 ♕g3+ ♔h7
> ½–½

An absolutely splendid example of mental cut and thrust, which does honour to both sides.

You should keep a record of your points scored on the table below so that you can add them up at the end of this book and calculate your exact chess strength.

Your points for this game.
Tick one of these:

2600 ☐		1800+ ☐	
2500+ ☐		1600+ ☐	
2400+ ☐		1400+ ☐	
2300+ ☐		1200+ ☐	
2200+ ☐		1000+ ☐	
2000+ ☐	less than 1000 ☐		

13

Short - Ljubojevic
Amsterdam 1991
Caro-Kann Defence

Your Target: 2600 points

Your partner is, for the third time, England's leading grandmaster Nigel Short. You have the white pieces and your opponent is the dangerous Yugoslav grandmaster Ljubomir Ljubojevic. If Nigel Short could win this game it would mean tournament victory in Amsterdam ahead of the world champion Gary Kasparov, so a tremendous effort is needed against a formidable opponent.

You will be posed a series of questions during this game each of which is announced by a diagram. Points will be awarded for the correct answer and there will also be bonus points available for seeing correctly into difficult variations. The maximum amount of points available for this game is 2600, equivalent to a world championship candidate. At each diagram where a question is posed (but not in the bonus variations) you may use your own discretion to award yourself 100 points if you do not find the move played but choose instead any other move that does not allow your opponent to capture material for no compensation or to checkmate you. For each diagram question, you may always use your discretion to award yourself 100 points for your chosen move unless there are clear instructions to the contrary.

As you play through the game use a sheet of paper to cover the page so that the test move under each diagram is not prematurely revealed.

	1	e4	c6
	2	d4	d5
	3	e5	

A favourite of Aron Nimzowitsch, the great chess thinker of the 1920s, and, as we saw in the previous game, a

move which has brought Short tremendous success in re-
cent tournaments.

	3	...	♗f5
	4	♘f3	e6
	5	♗e2	c5
	6	0-0	♘e7
	7	c3	♘ec6
	8	♗e3	♘d7
	9	a3	c4
	10	♘bd2	b5
	11	♘e1	h5
	12	g3	♗h3

Is this best? A bonus is available for the correct reply.

This move admits that Black will ultimately have to
trade off his queen's bishop for White's knight. Perhaps it
would have been better to maintain the bishop on the h7 -
b1 diagonal and then ultimately flee with the black king
to the relative safety of the queen's flank by means of ...
♘b6 and ... ♔d7. If you saw this defence award yourself
100 bonus points.

Now examine the diagram and try to guess White's next
move. Follow the same procedure throughout the rest of
the game, and look out for a bonus soon!

13 ♘g2

This move is obligatory. Award yourself *100 points* if
you played it. Deduct *400* for any other move.

13 ... g6

Perhaps 13 ... h4 deserved consideration here. If you did
in fact consider 13 ... h4 award yourself another *100 bonus.*

14 ♖e1 ♗xg2

15	♔xg2	♖b8
16	h3	a5
17	♘f3	♗e7
18	♕d2	♘b6
19	♘g5	♔f8

How does White now start his attack?

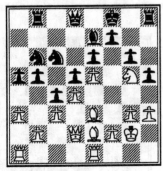

20 g4

300 points for this move. The battle lines have been clearly drawn. White plans to advance on the king's flank while Black is massing his forces for a queenside breakthrough. However, in this race between the two attacks Black is severely handicapped by the presence of his king in the firing line of White's aggression. For this reason, White's own attack soon gathers decisive momentum while Black's remains stillborn.

20	...	hxg4
21	hxg4	♔g7
22	♖h1	♕d7

How can White now feed more pieces into his already menacing attack?

23 ♗f4

This, in conjunction with Nigel's next move, forms the tremendously subtle introduction to a direct blitz against the black king. Give yourself *300 points* for this move.

        23 ...   ♖bf8
        24 ♕e3   ♕d8

White's pieces are on their best squares. How does he now break through?

25 ♘h7!!

A brilliant sacrificial irruption to seize control of the h-file with gain of tempo. If you found this move here, or were already considering it on moves 23 and 24, then give yourself *500 points*.

        25 ...   ♖xh7
        26 ♖xh7+   ♔xh7
        27 ♖h1+   ♔g8
        28 ♕h3   ♗h4

The only way to block the h-file.

Can White do better than to recapture the sacrificed piece?

29 ♗h6!

400 points for this move. 29 ♕xh4 is obvious but not nearly as strong since Black can exchange queens. In any case you should avoid 29 g5? ♔g7 30 ♕xh4 ♖h8 when Black repels the boarders. If you played 29 g5? deduct *100 points*.

29 ... g5

After 29 ... ♖e8 White has a sensational win with 30 g5 (this is now okay, since Black cannot get a rook to the h-file) 30 ... ♗xg5 31 f4!! ♗h4 32 ♗g5 and Black can resign. Award yourself *200 bonus points* if you saw this variation when considering your last move.

30 f4 gxf4

Can White do better than capture the rook?

31 ♗d1

300 points. Bringing round the reserves for the final onslaught, a manoeuvre which drives Black into some desperate sacrifices.

31	...	♘d7
32	♗c2	♘dxe5
33	dxe5	♘xe5
34	♗xf8	f3+
35	♔f1	♕g5

Think about White's alternatives here. There is a bonus coming.

36 ♕xh4

An alternative is 36 ♗h6 ♕xh6 37 g5 ♕xg5 38 ♖g1 winning Black's queen, but there is absolutely nothing wrong with the text, since Black only gets a couple of harmless checks. If you saw the variation starting 36 ♗h6 award yourself *100 bonus points*.

                        36 ...   ♛c1+
                        37 ♛e1

You must now consider what to do if Black plays 37 ...
♛xc2. What would you play here?

                        37 ...   ♛xe1+

Black had probably intended 37 ... ♛xc2 only too late
noticing the startling refutation 38 ♖h8+ ♚xh8 39 ♛xe5+
mating on g7. *200 extra bonus points* if you saw this.

                        38 ♚xe1   ♚xf8
                        39 g5   ♚g7
                        40 ♚f2   f5
                        41 ♖e1   ♞d3+
                        42 ♗xd3   cxd3
                        43 ♚xf3   1-0

Black resigns as he is hopelessly behind on material.

    You should keep a record of your points scored on the
table below so that you can add them up at the end of
this book and calculate your exact chess strength.

            Your points for this game.
            Tick one of these:

        2600   ☐   1800+ ☐
        2500+ ☐   1600+ ☐
        2400+ ☐   1400+ ☐
        2300+ ☐   1200+ ☐
        2200+ ☐   1000+ ☐
        2000+ ☐   less than 1000 ☐

14

Ivanchuk - Yudasin
Candidates' Match, Riga 1991
Queen's Indian Defence

Your Target: 2700 points

Your partner is the young Russian grandmaster Vasily Ivanchuk, widely tipped as a future world champion. You have the white pieces and your opponent is Leonid Yudasin. This game was played in Ivanchuk's virtual whitewash candidates' match victory during his first attempt on the world championship.

You will be posed a series of questions during this game each of which is announced by a diagram. Points will be awarded for the correct answer and there will also be bonus points available for seeing correctly into difficult variations. The maximum amount of points available for this game is 2700, equivalent to a potential future world champion. At each diagram where a question is posed (but not in the bonus variations) you may use your own discretion to award yourself 100 points if you do not find the move played but choose instead any other move that does not allow your opponent to capture material for no compensation or to checkmate you. For each diagram question, you may always use your discretion to award yourself 100 points for your chosen move unless there are clear instructions to the contrary.

As you play through the game use a sheet of paper to cover the page so that the test move under each diagram is not prematurely revealed.

1	d4	♘f6
2	c4	e6
3	♘f3	b6
4	g3	♗a6
5	b3	d5
6	♗g2	dxc4

An enterprising continuation which exposes Black to all sorts of dangers in the long diagonal. Nevertheless, the concept is fairly well tried and was used, for example, in one game between Karpov and Timman from their 1990 candidates' final.

7   ♘e5   ♗b4+

Now examine the diagram and try to guess White's next move. Follow the same procedure throughout the rest of the game.

8   ♔f1

300 points. White is forced into this somewhat uncomfortable contortion since other methods of parrying the check would allow Black to capture on d4 with his queen with generally unfortunate consequences for White. No points for anything else.

8   ...   ♘fd7

Which black unit should White now capture?

9   ♘xc4

200 points. If instead 9 ♘xd7 ♘xd7 10 ♗xa8 ♕xa8 then Black would have immense compensation for the loss of the exchange. Alternatively, though in this case Black's compensation is somewhat more opaque, 9 ♗xa8 ♘xe5 exploiting the pin in the d-file to regain some material. White players have almost universally shunned such complications, preferring to preserve the pressure exerted by the fianchettoed king's bishop rather than go for immediate material gain. If you appreciated all of this, namely how dangerous it is to win the exchange, award yourself *200 bonus points.*

9 ... c6
10 ♗b2 b5

Varying from 10 ... 0-0 11 ♘bd2 b5 12 ♘e3, as played in the Karpov - Timman game mentioned above.

11 ♘cd2 ♗b7
12 ♘c3 ♕b6

Black's strategy stands or falls by his ability to achieve the freeing thrust ... c5. White's next move, and the manoeuvre which follows it, prevents Black's desired advance for some time to come.

13 ♘ce4 0-0

Black dare not play 13 ... c5, which would open the diagonal for White's queen's bishop. However, after the text move, White immediately sets up an iron grip over the c5-square. How does he do it?

14 a3

300 points, but only if you have already planned to follow up with b4. Otherwise take the standard *100 points*, usually on offer for reasonable alternatives.

14 ... ♗e7
15 b4 a5

White must now deal with the attack against his b4-

pawn. How?

16   ♘c5

200 points. The culmination of White's strategic ambitions. Black is now permanently fettered on the queen's wing and his queen's bishop is a miserable sight, imprisoned as it is by its own pawns.

16   ...   ♖d8

What is the best way for White to complete his development?

17   ♗f3

200 points. To free the g2-square for his king so that he can connect his rooks.

17   ...   axb4
18   axb4   ♘a6

At last Black succeeds in developing his queen's knight but not to a very impressive square.

19   ♕b3   e5

Black must do something to shake White's control even though this course is risky.

How does White react?

20 ⟋xb7!

200 points. A surprising but excellent choice. The point of Ivanchuk's play is that he can now transfer the centre of gravity towards Black's depleted king's flank.

20 ...   ♛xb7

There is a bonus coming if you can see how Ivanchuk plans to meet a black capture of his b4-pawn.

21 dxe5   ⟋b6

If 21 ... ⟋xb4 22 e6 disrupts Black's kingside while if instead 21 ... ♝xb4 22 ♖xa6 ♝xd2 23 ♖xc6 and wins. *200 bonus points* for seeing all of this.

22 ⟋e4   ⟋d5

Black is determined to capture on b4 but he also wants to prevent the dangerous thrust e6. Therefore, he closes the diagonal of White's queen before harvesting the pawn.

23 ♔g2   ♝xb4

In fact 23 ... ⟋axb4 would be stronger.

24 ♖ac1   ♛b6

Now three hammer blows follow, over the next three moves which destroy the black position. What are they?

25 ♕c2!

300 points. A tremendously subtle move. It would at first appear that White's ambitions are directed entirely against Black's weak pawn on c6, but White has a much more devastating plan in view after Black's natural response.

25 ...   ♖ac8

What is White's next move?

26 ♘g5

200 points. White's true plans are at last revealed. Black has absolutely no defence to this sudden switch of fronts against his king.

26 ...   g6

Now, what did White play?

27 e6

200 points. Wrenching open the diagonal towards Black's king. There is a bonus available if you can refute Black's main defence.

27 ...   fxe6

Black is quite without defence. If 27 ... f6 28 ♗xd5 ♖xd5

29 ♘e4 or 28 ... cxd5 29 ♕xc8 ♖xc8 30 ♖xc8+ ♔g7 31 ♖hc1 d4 32 ♖1c6 ♕b7 33 ♗xd4 and Black can resign. *200 bonus points* for seeing all of this.

28 ♕e4   1-0

He is without resource against the threats of 29 ♕xe6+ or 29 ♕e5.

You should keep a record of your points scored on the table below so that you can add them up at the end of this book and calculate your exact chess strength.

Your points for this game.
Tick one of these:

2700	☐	1800+	☐
2600+	☐	1600+	☐
2500+	☐	1400+	☐
2400+	☐	1200+	☐
2300+	☐	1000+	☐
2200+	☐	less than 1000	☐
2000+	☐		

15

Tal - Smyslov
Bled 1959
Caro-Kann Defence

Your Target: 2700 points

Your partner is Mikhail Tal, at the time this game was played a grandmaster, but soon to become world champion. Your opponent (Black) is Vasily Smyslov, world champion himself from 1957 – 1958. When Tal played this game he was on the way to his own world championship challenge against the mighty Botvinnik, and Tal had to win here to keep his chances of qualifying alive for the world title match.

You will be posed a series of questions during this game each of which is announced by a diagram. Points will be awarded for the correct answer and there will also be bonus points available for seeing correctly into difficult variations. The maximum amount of points available for this game is 2700, equivalent to a potential future world champion. At each diagram where a question is posed (but not in the bonus variations) you may use your own discretion to award yourself 100 points if you do not find the move played but choose instead any other move that does not allow your opponent to capture material for no compensation or to checkmate you. For each diagram question, you may always use your discretion to award yourself 100 points for your chosen move unless there are clear instructions to the contrary.

As you play through the game use a sheet of paper to cover the page so that the test move under each diagram is not prematurely revealed.

1	e4	c6
2	d3	d5
3	♘d2	e5
4	♘gf3	

A most unusual method of countering the solid Caro-Kann.

$$4 \quad \ldots \quad ♘d7$$
$$5 \quad d4$$

Sacrificing a tempo is justified in view of the passive placing of Black's queen's knight. White now obtains a superb development.

$$5 \quad \ldots \quad dxe4$$
$$6 \quad ♘xe4 \quad exd4$$

Now examine the diagram and try to guess White's next move. Follow the same procedure throughout the rest of the game.

$$7 \quad ♕xd4$$

200 points. Much the superior recapture, seizing a key central station for White's most powerful piece without any fear of molestation.

$$7 \quad \ldots \quad ♘gf6$$
$$8 \quad ♗g5 \quad ♗e7$$

Which way should Tal now choose to further his mobilization?

9 0-0-0

150 points. The watchword is swift development of White's forces.

9 ... 0-0

Now, what did White play?

10 ♘d6

300 points. White has free play for his pieces and is in complete possession of the central files. His knight at d6 dominates the board and it is quite natural that Tal soon turns his attention towards a sacrificial solution. You should now keep your eyes open for the manifold complex variations which will soon arise and which carry with them valuable bonus points.

10 ... ♕a5
11 ♗c4 b5

The white king's bishop is attacked. Should it retreat and, if so, where to?

12 ♗d2

150 points. Driving back the black queen but, as we shall soon see, there is also a deeper point to this retreat of the other bishop.

12 ... ♛a6

The question remains, what should Tal do about his king's bishop?

13 ♘f5

150 points. Gaining a tempo against the black king's bishop so that the knight can press against the g7-pawn, a critical defender in front of the black king.

13 ... ♝d8

Can White still afford to offer his king's bishop to the black pawn?

14 ♛h4!

400 points. The retreat 14 ♝b3 would, in fact, permit Black to free himself with 14 ... c5, threatening ... c4 to crowd White's bishop out of play. Instead, Tal decides to take Black's king's fortress by storm, whatever the cost in material.

14 ... bxc4

How does White justify his sacrifice? Think in detail about variations, since there are huge bonuses imminent!

15 ♕g5

150 points. Threatening mate on g7 was behind White's previous move 14 ♕h4. We also comprehend now why White's bishop retreated from g5 to d2, to make way for the advent of the white queen. Think carefully about Black's best defence before looking at the next note.

15 ...   ♘h5

Returning the piece to alleviate the attack. 15 ... ♘e8 16 ♕xd8 ♘ef6 17 ♕a5 favours White, due to his sounder pawns in the endgame but the most intricate defence to White's brutal threat of ♕xg7 mate is 15 ... g6. In that case, however, White would play 16 ♘h6+ ♔g7 17 ♗c3 ♕xa2 18 ♘h4 ♕a1+ 19 ♔d2 ♕a6 20 ♘(h4)f5+ ♔h8 21 ♘d6 ♔g7 22 ♖fe1 c5 23 ♘(h6)f5+ ♔g8 24 ♕h6 gxf5 25 ♕g5+ ♔h8 26 ♘xf5 ♖g8 27 ♖e8 and wins. Award yourself up to *500 bonus points* depending on how much of this was foreseen.

16 ♘h6+   ♔h8
17 ♕xh5   ♕xa2

If 17 ... gxh6 18 ♗c3+ f6 19 ♕xh6 ♖g8 20 ♘g5. *150 bonus points* for seeing this. What is White's next move?

18   ♗c3

200 points. This move kills two birds with one stone. It stops Black's mating threats and presses towards the vulnerable g7-pawn in the black camp.

18   ...   ♘f6

Smyslov cracks under the pressure. He had to play 18 ... ♗f6. Why is Smyslov's choice a disaster?

19   ♕xf7!!

350 points. A beautiful move which immediately terminates the game. If 19 ... ♖xf7 20 ♖xd8+ followed by checkmate or 19 ... ♖e8 20 ♕g8+ and however Black captures 21 ♘f7 is smothered mate.

19   ...   ♕a1+
20   ♔d2   ♖xf7
21   ♘xf7+   ♔g8
22   ♖xa1   ♔xf7
23   ♘e5+   ♔e6

The upshot is, Black loses too much material and can resign with a clear conscience.

24   ♘xc6   ♘e4+
25   ♔e3   ♗b6+
26   ♗d4   1-0

A remarkable game, typical of Tal's dazzling sacrificial style.

You should keep a record of your points scored on the table below so that you can add them up at the end of this book and calculate your exact chess strength.

Your points for this game.
Tick one of these:

2700	☐	1800+	☐
2600+	☐	1600+	☐
2500+	☐	1400+	☐
2400+	☐	1200+	☐
2300+	☐	1000+	☐
2200+	☐	less than 1000	☐
2000+	☐		

16

Tal - Panno
Buenos Aires 1991
Sicilian Defence

Your Target: 2700 points

Your partner is the brilliant former world champion Mikhail Tal, who held the supreme title in 1960/61. You have the white pieces and your opponent is Oscar Panno, the Argentine grandmaster.

You will be posed a series of questions during this game each of which is announced by a diagram. Points will be awarded for the correct answer and there will also be bonus points available for seeing correctly into difficult variations. The maximum amount of points available for this game is 2700, equivalent to a potential future world champion. At each diagram where a question is posed (but not in the bonus variations) you may use your own discretion to award yourself 100 points if you do not find the move played but choose instead any other move that does not allow your opponent to capture material for no compensation or to checkmate you. For each diagram question, you may always use your discretion to award yourself 100 points for your chosen move unless there are clear instructions to the contrary.

As you play through the game use a sheet of paper to cover the page so that the test move under each diagram is not prematurely revealed.

1	e4	c5
2	♘f3	e6
3	♘c3	a6
4	d4	cxd4
5	♘xd4	♛c7
6	♗d3	♘c6
7	♗e3	♘f6
8	0-0	♘e5

| 9 | h3 | ♝c5 |

This is a well-known position from the Sicilian Defence. In fact the game Tal – Najdorf, USSR v The World, Belgrade 1970, reached exactly the same position. Then Tal chose 10 ♕e2. Now he tries to improve White's play, offering a pawn sacrifice which, if declined, leaves White with a distinct spatial advantage.

| 10 | ♘a4 | ♝a7 |

Now examine the diagram and try to guess White's next move. Follow the same procedure throughout the rest of the game.

| 11 | c4 |

200 points. What happens if Black now captures on c4? Try to work out the variations now since there are some valuable bonus points available.

The variations are extraordinarily interesting: 11 ... ♘xc4 12 ♝xc4 (Not 12 ♖c1? ♘xe3) 12 ... ♕xc4 13 ♖c1 ♕b4 14 ♘xe6!! This move is the key to White's advantage. For example 14 ... dxe6 15 ♝xa7 ♝d7 16 ♝c5 ♕xa4 17 ♕d6 ♔d8 18 ♕e7+ ♔c7 19 ♝b6+ ♔xb6 20 ♕c5 mate.

If after 14 ♘xe6 Black decides to reject the sacrifice with 14 ... ♝xe3 then 15 ♘c7+ ♔d8 16 fxe3 ♖b8 17 e5 ♘e8 18 ♘d5 ♕e4 19 ♘ab6 ♖f8 20 ♖c4 ♕xe5 21 ♕a4 ♕e6 22 ♕a5 leads to a clearly winning position for White. Up to *200 bonus points* depending on how much of this you saw.

| 11 | ... | d6 |

The Argentine grandmaster prefers a cautious path.

12	♖c1	♝d7
13	♘c3	♘xd3
14	♕xd3	0-0

What did White play now?

15   ♖fd1

150 points. Storing up energy in the d-file against Black's backward pawn on d6, which will be weakened by the impending exchange of dark-squared bishops.

15   ...   ♖fc8
16   b3   ♘e8
17   ♘f3   ♗xe3
18   ♕xe3   b6

Black has survived the hidden hazards of the opening and now looks forward to a quiet middlegame where he is slightly cramped but extremely solid and can operate with freeing threats such as ... b5. Tal's task now is to generate a direct attack before Black can consolidate. How?

19   ♕f4

150 points. Gaining maximum manoeuvring space for White's queen.

19   ...   ♗c6

How can White now threaten Black's seemingly impenetrable fortress?

20 ♘b5

500 points. A standard but most important tactical device which maintains White's initiative. If 20 ... axb5 21 cxb5 regains the material as a result of the pin on the c-file.

   20 ...   ♗xb5
   21 cxb5   ♛b7
   22 ♖xc8   ♖xc8

Which move is best for retaining White's slight initiative?

23 e5

200 points. White must continue to go on the offensive in order to extract the maximum advantage from his marginally superior mobility and more effective development.

   23 ...   dxe5
   24 ♘xe5

Now think very carefully - before reading the rest of this note - about how Black should be defending the position. A substantial bonus is coming up. White's attack, with threats such as ♖d7, has reached its zenith. Important in what follows is the fact that White has gained freedom for his king with the move h3 from back rank threats, while Black is still continually subject to such problems. The critical line here is 24 ... f6 25 ♕g4 fxe5 26 ♕xe6+ ♔h8 27 ♖d7 ♕e4 28 ♖f7 which attacks the rook on c8 and threatens ♖f8 mate. Black has no defence. Up to *200 bonus points* depending on how much of this you saw.

	24	...	♘f6
	25	bxa6	♕xa6
	26	♘c6	♖e8

What next for White?

27 ♕c7

250 points. Preparing a neat exploitation of the back rank theme. Watch out for bonus points very soon.

27 ... ♕e2

If instead 27 ... ♘d5 28 ♘e7+ ♘xe7 29 ♖d8 ♔f8 30 ♕d7 wins, or 27 ... ♘d5 28 ♘e7+ ♖xe7 29 ♕xe7 ♘xe7 30 ♖d8 mate. *300 bonus points* if you saw both lines. What now?

28 ☐d8

200 points. The only way to progress, as you will probably have guessed from the previous note, is to try to cause Black problems with back rank mating traps.

28 ...   ♕e1+
29 ♔h2   ♕xf2

Can Tal avoid a perpetual check draw to his own king and still continue his own attacking schemes?

30 ♘e5!

150 points. Brilliantly continuing the attack.

30 ...   ♕f4+

In trying to get a draw by perpetual check with his queen against White's king, Panno falls into one of the many pitfalls. This leads to a clear loss as Black is now obliged to give up his queen to stave off checkmate. The last possible defensive try is 30 ... ♔h8.

31 ♔g1   ♕e3+

At first glance, it looks as if White may not be able to escape from the checks.

32 ♔h1   ♕e1+
33 ♔h2   ♕xe5+

But now all is clear. The checks have run out and White's manifold threats make it absolutely apparent that this self-immolation of the queen is the only way to survive for a couple of moves.

34 ♕xe5   ☐xd8
35 ♕c7   ☐e8
36 ♕xb6   1-0

There is a bonus for working out how White copes with 36 ... e5 and the advance of Black's passed pawn - had Panno chosen to continue playing. Can you work this out?

The win goes 36 ... e5 37 a4 e4 38 ♔g1 e3 39 ♔f1 e2+ 40 ♔e1 when Black's passed pawn is blockaded while White will easily promote a queenside pawn. *200 bonus points* for seeing this, namely, how White promotes a pawn, while simultaneously blocking Black's passed pawn with his king.

You should keep a record of your points scored on the table below so that you can add them up at the end of this book and calculate your exact chess strength.

Your points for this game.
Tick one of these:

2700	☐	1800+	☐
2600+	☐	1600+	☐
2500+	☐	1400+	☐
2400+	☐	1200+	☐
2300+	☐	1000+	☐
2200+	☐	less than 1000	☐
2000+	☐		

17 Spassky - Unzicker
Santa Monica 1966
Ruy Lopez

Your Target: 2700 points

Your partner is Boris Spassky, world champion from 1969 to 1972. You have the white pieces and your opponent is the German grandmaster Wolfgang Unzicker. In the tournament where this game was played Spassky was involved in a thrilling race for first prize with Bobby Fischer and he had to win this game in order to stay ahead.

You will be posed a series of questions during this game each of which is announced by a diagram. Points will be awarded for the correct answer and there will also be bonus points available for seeing correctly into difficult variations. The maximum amount of points available for this game is 2700, equivalent to a potential future world champion. At each diagram where a question is posed (but not in the bonus variations) you may use your own discretion to award yourself 100 points if you do not find the move played but choose instead any other move that does not allow your opponent to capture material for no compensation or to checkmate you. For each diagram question, you may always use your discretion to award yourself 100 points for your chosen move unless there are clear instructions to the contrary.

As you play through the game use a sheet of paper to cover the page so that the test move under each diagram is not prematurely revealed.

	1	e4	e5
	2	♘f3	♘c6
	3	♗b5	a6

Black does not fear 4 ♗xc6 dxc6 5 ♘xe5 on account of 5 ... ♕g5 forking the white knight on e5 and the pawn on g2. For that reason, Black's third move invariably leads to the closed heavyweight positions which exhibit the strategic nuances of the main lines of the Ruy Lopez.

4	♗a4	♞f6
5	0-0	♗e7
6	♖e1	b5
7	♗b3	d6
8	c3	0-0
9	h3	♞b8

This retreat may appear strange but it is well founded. The black knight will reposition itself on d7 in order to strengthen Black's pawn at e5. Meanwhile, Black frees his c7-pawn for future thrusts against the white centre. 9 ... ♗b7 10 d4 ♖e8 11 ♞bd2 ♗f8 12 a4 h6 13 ♗c2 exd4 14 cxd4 ♞b4 15 ♗b1, as in numerous Kasparov – Karpov games, is an alternative.

10	d4	♞bd7
11	♞bd2	♗b7
12	♗c2	♖e8

Also possible is 12 ... c5, e.g. 13 d5 g6 14 ♞f1 ♞h5 15 ♗h6 ♞g7 16 ♞e3 ♞f6 as in Karpov – Gligoric, Leningrad Interzonal 1973.

13	♞f1	♗f8
14	♞g3	g6
15	♗g5	h6
16	♗d2	♗g7
17	♖c1	c5

Now examine the diagram and try to guess White's next move. Follow the same procedure throughout the rest of the game.

18	d5

400 points. A typical situation has arisen for the Ruy

Lopez, one that is extremely instructive in teaching the best ways to handle such positions. White now blocks the centre and guides the game into a period of long strategic manoeuvres. White's long-range goal is to utilise his slight superiority in terrain in order to concentrate his forces on the weakest portion of Black's defences.

	18	...	♘b6

This turns out to be a waste of time. An improvement would have been 18 ... c4 followed immediately by ... ♘c5.

19	♗d3	♛c7
20	♘h2	♘a4
21	♖b1	c4
22	♗c2	♘c5

How does Spassky prepare further for his attack?

	23	♘g4

400 points. A crucial preparation for White's attack.

23	...	♚h7
24	♛f3	♘xg4
25	hxg4	♛e7

What did White play now?

26 b3

300 points. A subtle move, the point of which is to force an exchange of pawns and thus deprive the black knight of its outpost on d3.

26	...	cxb3
27	axb3	♘f6
28	♘f1	♗g5
29	♘e3	♗c8

Should White now continue the attack on the kingside, or the queenside, and how?

30 g3

150 points. Making way for White's king so that the rook can reach its optimum attacking post on h1.

30	...	♘d7
31	♕e2	♘f6
32	f3	h5
33	♔g2	♕d8
34	♖h1	♔g8

Can White break through at once, or must he first prepare some more?

35 ♖bf1

150 points. Planning to meet 35 ... ♗xe3 36 ♗xe3 hxg4
with 37 ♗g5 gxf3+ 38 ♕xf3 with an obviously winning
attack. The strategic point of this move is to place the
rook on a file that may become opened in the vicinity of
the black king.

35 ... ♗h6

Spassky has inexorably built up his forces for a decisive
onslaught against the black king and now he is ready to
break down the barricades, the question is how?

36 ♘f5‼

550 points. A beautiful sacrifice which decides the
battle. Obviously if 36 ... gxf5 37 ♗xh6, with the threat of
♗g5, would win easily. This knight thrust is highly intricate, so watch out for bonus points for correctly seeing
into difficult variations over the next few moves.

36 ... ♗xd2
37 ♕xd2 gxf5

Acquiescing in his fate. If instead 37 ... ♘h7 38 ♕h6 ♕f6
39 g5 ♕h8 40 ♘xd6 ♖d8 41 ♘f5 gxf5 42 ♖xh5 ♕g7 43 ♕b6
♗d7 44 ♖fh1 ♘f8 45 ♕f6 ♘g6 46 exf5 and White wins. Up
to *300 bonus points* depending on how much of this you
saw.

38 ♕h6 fxg4
39 fxg4 ♗xg4

Black is forced to return the piece for if 39 ... ♘xg4 40
♕xh5 ♘e3+ 41 ♔g1 and mate soon follows. *300 bonus
points* if you saw this.

40 ♖xf6 ♕e7
41 ♕g5+ ♔f8

How does White finish off?

42 ♗d1

150 points. The final link in White's attacking chain, to knock out the defender of the h5-pawn.

42	... ♗xd1
43	♖xd1 ♖ec8
44	♖df1 ♖xc3
45	♕xh5 ♖c2+
46	♔h1 1-0

A most elegantly conducted victory against a solid opponent.

You should keep a record of your points scored on the table below so that you can add them up at the end of this book and calculate your exact chess strength.

Your points for this game.
Tick one of these:

2700	☐	1800+	☐
2600+	☐	1600+	☐
2500+	☐	1400+	☐
2400+	☐	1200+	☐
2300+	☐	1000+	☐
2200+	☐	less than 1000	☐
2000+	☐		

Alekhine - Bogolyubov
Cracow 1941
Catalan Opening

Your Target: 2700 points

Your partner is the former world champion Alexander Alekhine. Your opponent is the redoubtable Efim Bogolyubov, the only man to have held the German and Soviet championships simultaneously.

You will be posed a series of questions during this game each of which is announced by a diagram. Points will be awarded for the correct answer and there will also be bonus points available for seeing correctly into difficult variations. The maximum amount of points available for this game is 2700, equivalent to a potential future world champion. At each diagram where a question is posed (but not in the bonus variations) you may use your own discretion to award yourself 100 points if you do not find the move played but choose instead any other move that does not allow your opponent to capture material for no compensation or to checkmate you. For each diagram question, you may always use your discretion to award yourself 100 points for your chosen move unless there are clear instructions to the contrary.

As you play through the game use a sheet of paper to cover the page so that the test move under each diagram is not prematurely revealed.

1	d4	e6
2	c4	♘f6
3	♘f3	d5
4	g3	♗e7
5	♗g2	0-0
6	0-0	♘bd7
7	♕c2	dxc4

Alekhine was a pioneer of the subtle Catalan system in

which White hopes to exert subtle probing pressure against Black's pawns on the queen's flank.

8	♘bd2	c5
9	♘xc4	cxd4
10	♘xd4	♘b6
11	♘xb6	♛xb6
12	♗e3	♗c5

Now examine the diagram and try to guess White's next move. Follow the same procedure throughout the rest of the game.

13 ♘f5

200 points. A highly refined method of forcing the trade of Black's active dark squared bishop. Of course 13 ... exf5 would now fail miserably to 14 ♗xc5. Alekhine's games bristle with tactical shots of this nature and you should constantly be on the look-out for them.

13	...	♗xe3
14	♘xe3	♗d7
15	♛b3	♗b5

Before reading the remainder of this note, ask yourself whether Black's 15th move is his best defence. A bonus hangs on this.

After this plausible attempt Black is condemned to almost eternal suffering, since he can never quite eradicate White's slight initiative. Correct would have been 15 ... ♛xb3 16 axb3 ♗c6 17 ♗xc6 bxc6 when the mutual weaknesses in pawn structure would more or less have cancelled each other out. Award yourself a bonus of *200 points* if you appreciated that this would have been Black's best defence. How should White now react to the threat to his e-pawn?

16 ♖fc1

400 points. So often in chess it is difficult to tell which rook, the king's or the queen's, to move to an open file. Ordinarily, one would like to play 16 ♖ac1 here so that the white king's rook would later have the opportunity to operate in the open d-file. However, 16 ♖ac1 does not address the question of the vulnerability of white's pawn on e2. Indeed, 16 ♖ac1 fails to 16 ... ♗xe2 17 ♕xb6 axb6 when the white rook on f1 is attacked and the pawn on a2 is hanging. In contradistinction after 16 ♖fc1 ♗xe2 17 ♕xb6 axb6 White can play 18 ♗xb7 with a clear conscience. He would then have the advantage of a two to one majority of pawns on the queen's wing. *150 bonus points* if you saw this variation and the general justification for it.

	16	...	♖ad8
	17	♘c4	♕a6
	18	a4	♗c6
	19	♗xc6	♕xc6
	20	♘e3	♕d7

Now, how did White proceed?

21   ♖c4

150 points. Correctly utilising his asset and preparing to double rooks in the open file which he controls.

21	...	♖c8
22	♖d1	♕e7
23	♖dc1	♖xc4
24	♕xc4	h6

White now enjoys a clear advantage based on his domination of the open c-file. How best to exploit this?

25   a5

200 points. Not 25 ♕c7 at once on account of the counter-attack 25 ... ♕b4! and Black has considerably freed his game. Nothing for 25 ♕c7?

25	...	♖d8
26	♕c7	

This penetration of the black position by the white queen is now correct since the black queen's freedom of movement is restricted by its obligation to defend the black rook.

26	...	♔f8
27	♔g2	♔e8

Should Bogolyubov have traded queens? A bonus hinges on the answer.

Alekhine himself wrote of this position: "One can understand that the endgame after 27 ... ♕xc7 28 ♖xc7 ♖d7 29 ♖c8+ ♔e7 30 ♖a8 does not appeal to Black; but the king is too vulnerable in the middlegame and it is therefore questionable whether simplification would not have been advisable all the same." *A bonus of 150* is available here if you saw this.

How does White make progress? Black's position

seems compact enough.

28 ♕e5

300 points. Alekhine had hinted that White now wanted to keep queens on the board and this is the most active way of so doing.

28	...	♕d6
29	♕b5+	♕d7
30	♕b3	♖c8
31	♘c4	♕d5+
32	f3	♔f8
33	♕a3+	♔g8

The crisis has been reached and White's next move can decide the game. What is it?

34 ♘b6!!

400 points. A neat tactical blow which ensures the win either of the exchange or of Black's queen for rook and knight. This tactical solution arising from what had seemed a dry position is typical Alekhine. If now 34 ... axb6 35 ♖xc8+ wins, or 34 ... ♕d8 35 ♖xc8 is decisive.

34	...	♖xc1

35	♘xd5	♘xd5
36	e4	♖c2+
37	♔h3	♘f6

What did White play now?

38 ♕d6

200 points. So often, players throw away the fruit of fine strategy by inaccuracies in the technical phase. Here, Alekhine must combine threats against the black queenside pawns with defence of his own king, which is somewhat boxed in. At every stage his move is the most accurate possible and the technical conclusion is a joy to watch. Watch out for an imminent bonus.

| | 38 ... | g5 |

If 38 ... ♖xb2 39 ♕b8+ ♔h7 40 a6 wins. *150 bonus points.*

39	♕d3	♖c6
40	♕d4	♔g7
41	♕xa7	h5
42	♕xb7	♖c2

How does the white king escape from Black's sudden counter-attacking net of pawns?

43 g4

200 points. The last really difficult move of the game. Having captured Black's queenside pawns with his queen White must ensure that his own king has sufficient space and does not get trapped by the advancing black g- and h-pawns.

43	...	♞h7
44	♕b3	hxg4+
45	fxg4	♖e2
46	♕d3	♖f2
47	♕d4+	♖f6
48	a6	♞f8
49	a7	♞g6
50	♕xf6+	1-0

You should keep a record of your points scored on the table below so that you can add them up at the end of this book and calculate your exact chess strength.

Your points for this game.
Tick one of these:

2700	☐		1800+	☐
2600+	☐		1600+	☐
2500+	☐		1400+	☐
2400+	☐		1200+	☐
2300+	☐		1000+	☐
2200+	☐	less than 1000	☐
2000+	☐			

I conclude this book with a real treat, two games by world champion Gary Kasparov against his two possible rivals for the world crown in 1993, Jan Timman and Nigel Short.

19 Kasparov - Timman
London 1984
Queen's Gambit Declined
Your Target: 2800 points

Your partner is Gary Kasparov, the highest-ranked player in the history of chess! You have the white pieces and your opponent is Jan Timman, Holland's best grandmaster and for many years the most highly-ranked player outside the USSR.

You will be posed a series of questions during this game each of which is announced by a diagram. Points will be awarded for the correct answer and there will also be bonus points available for seeing correctly into difficult variations. The maximum amount of points available for this game is 2800, equivalent to a super world champion. At each diagram where a question is posed (but not in the bonus variations) you may use your own discretion to award yourself 100 points if you do not find the move played but choose instead any other move that does not allow your opponent to capture material for no compensation or to checkmate you. For each diagram question, you may always use your discretion to award yourself 100 points for your chosen move unless there are clear instructions to the contrary.

As you play through the game use a sheet of paper to cover the page so that the test move under each diagram is not prematurely revealed.

1	d4	♘f6
2	c4	e6
3	♘f3	d5
4	♘c3	♗e7
5	♗g5	0-0
6	e3	h6
7	♗xf6	♗xf6

8 ♕c2

The Tartakower Variation of the Queen's Gambit Declined, as seen here, was to figure heavily in the subsequent matches between Karpov and Kasparov for the world title. Strangely, in spite of his success in this game, Kasparov never tried 8 ♕c2 against Karpov, although he did go in for 8 ♕b3 and 8 ♖c1. Karpov himself played 8 ♕c2 in one game from their 1985 match - a game which White won.

8 ... c5

The natural reaction to free his position, although it does leave Black with some weaknesses in the centre. In Karpov - Kasparov, game 4, Moscow 1985, Kasparov played 8 ... ♘a6 but never completely equalised.

9 dxc5 ♕a5
10 cxd5 exd5
11 0-0-0 ♗e6

Watch out for a bonus on Black's next move.

12 ♘xd5 ♖c8

If 12 ... ♗xd5 13 ♖xd5 ♕xa2 14 ♗c4 ♕a1+ 15 ♕b1 ♕a4 16 ♕a2 ♕xa2 17 ♗xa2 ♘a6 18 ♔b1 with some advantage to White whose light-squared bishop can become annoyingly active. If Black tries to trade it off with ... ♘b4 White has time to penetrate to the seventh rank with his rook. Give yourself a bonus of up to *300 points* depending on how much of this you saw.

Now examine the diagram and try to guess White's next move. Follow the same procedure throughout the rest of the game.

13 ♔b1

300 points. 13 ♘xf6+ gxf6 shattering Black's kingside

pawns is superficially attractive, but given the danger to White's king and queen in the soon to be opened c-file 13 ♔b1 is forced. Do not give yourself credit for any alternative, but watch out for another bonus on Black's next move.

	13 ...	♗xd5

On 13 ... ♖xc5 White has 14 b4! ♖xc2 15 ♘xf6+ gxf6 16 bxa5 with the threat of ♖d8+. *200 bonus points* for seeing this.

	14	♖xd5	♘c6
	15	♗c4	♘b4
	16	♕d2	

Pinning Black's knight and thus maintaining his material advantage.

	16	...	♖xc5
	17	♖xc5	♕xc5

How should White meet the threats of ... ♕xc4 and ... ♕f5+?

	18	♖c1!

150 points. The point of this move is to prevent 18 ... ♕f5+ 19 ♔a1 ♘c2+; to seize an open file; and finally, to set up some traps against the black queen. The upshot of the opening is that White has won a pawn for which Black has some pressure against White's slightly exposed king. What Black plays now, though, is an error which permits White to continually gain ground by threatening to exchange queens. Best is 18 ... ♕e7 though not, of course, 18 ... ♖d8 on account of 19 ♕xd8+ ♗xd8 20 ♗xf7+ ♔xf7 21 ♖xc5. Award yourself up to *150 bonus points* depending on how much of this you saw.

	18	...	♕b6?

This is the losing move but it takes some very fine play on Kasparov's part to prove it. Timman was probably relying on his threats against White's king focusing on the b2-pawn.

White now has a strong but apparently risky-looking stroke. What is it?

19 ♕d7!!

350 points. The theme is a massive punch against f7. Look carefully now, before proceeding, at how to deal with Black's possibilities of counter-attack. There is a huge bonus coming depending on how deeply you see into this position. It looks as if Black should now play 19 ... ♘xa2, ignoring the threat against f7 and creating a threat of checkmate himself against White's b2-pawn. Nevertheless, in that case White has a beautiful win based on his hegemony over the light squares, namely 20 ♖c2 ♖d8 21 ♕xf7+ ♔h7 22 ♔xa2 ♕a5+ 23 ♔b1 ♖d1+ 24 ♖c1 ♕f5+ 25 e4 ♕xe4+ 26 ♔a2 ♖xc1 27 ♕g8+ ♔g6 28 ♗f7+ ♔f5 29 ♕h7+ ♔f4 30 g3+ ♔xf3 31 ♗h5+ and White wins. At the start of this variation, if Black meets 20 ♖c2 with 20 ... ♘c3+ then 21 ♔c1 ♘e4 22 ♗xf7+ ♔h8 23 ♘e5!! ♗xe5 24 ♖c8+ leading to mate. Now award yourself up to a massive maximum of *650 bonus points* depending on how much of these variations you saw when choosing 19 ♕d7.

	19	...	**♖f8**
	20	**♕b5**	**♕d6**
	21	**e4**	**♘c6**

The storm has passed, and White's task is slightly easier. Nevertheless, great accuracy is still required against Black's dark-squared counterplay. How did Kasparov squash it?

22   ♗d5

150 points. Centralising the bishop and shutting Black's queen out of play.

22   ...   a6
23   ♕xb7   ♘e5

Not 23 ... ♖b8 24 ♖xc6 ♖xb7 25 ♖xd6 ♖xb2+ 26 ♔c1 winning. What is White's next move?

24   ♖c8

125 points. Once more, the light squares are paramount in that 24 ... ♘xf3 is refuted by 25 ♕xf7+. *125 bonus points* for seeing this.

24   ...   ♖xc8
25   ♕xc8+   ♔h7

Watch out for a bonus soon.

26   ♕c2   ♔g8

If Black could now play 26 ... ♘xf3 27 gxf3 he would have some drawing chances in spite of his two pawn deficit but in fact 27 e5+ wins on the spot. *150 bonus points* for seeing this,

27   ♘d2   g5

	28	a3	♔g7
	29	♘f1	♕b6
	30	♘g3	♔g6
	31	♔a2	h5
	32	♕c8	h4
	33	♕g8+	♗g7

What now is the *mot juste*?

34 ♘h5

150 points. If 34 ... ♔xh5 35 ♕xg7 is hopeless for Black. Therefore ...

1-0

You should keep a record of your points scored on the table below so that you can add them up at the end of this book and calculate your exact chess strength.

Your points for this game.
Tick one of these:

2800 ☐	2000+ ☐
2700+ ☐	1800+ ☐
2600+ ☐	1600+ ☐
2500+ ☐	1400+ ☐
2400+ ☐	1200+ ☐
2300+ ☐	1000+ ☐
2200+ ☐	less than 1000 ☐

Kasparov - Short
Linares 1990
English Opening

Your Target: 2800 points

Your partner is again world champion Gary Kasparov. You have the white pieces and your opponent is grandmaster Nigel Short, England's best ever prospect to become world champion.

You will be posed a series of questions during this game each of which is announced by a diagram. Points will be awarded for the correct answer and there will also be bonus points available for seeing correctly into difficult variations. The maximum amount of points available for this game is 2800, equivalent to a record-breaking world champion. At each diagram where a question is posed (but not in the bonus variations) you may use your own discretion to award yourself 100 points if you do not find the move played but choose instead any other move that does not allow your opponent to capture material for no compensation or to checkmate you. For each diagram question, you may always use your discretion to award yourself 100 points for your chosen move unless there are clear instructions to the contrary.

As you play through the game use a sheet of paper to cover the page so that the test move under each diagram is not prematurely revealed.

1	c4	e5
2	♘c3	♘c6
3	g3	g6
4	♗g2	♗g7
5	d3	d6
6	e4	♗e6
7	♘ge2	♕d7
8	♘d5	

This, combined with White's next, represents a some-what artificial continuation which poses Black few problems in his path to equality. Preferable would be 8 ♗e3.

8	...	♘ce7
9	d4	c6
10	♘e3	♗h3

Now examine the diagram and try to guess White's next move. Follow the same procedure throughout the rest of the game.

11 0–0

150 points. White should, in fact, play 11 ♗xh3 ♕xh3 12 d5 pushing forward in the centre. If you chose this instead of Kasparov's move, give yourself *200 points.* After the text Black can start a dangerous attack.

11	...	♗xg2
12	♔xg2	exd4
13	♘xd4	h5

How should White react to this attack?

14 a4

150 points. White has not handled the opening particularly well and this is part of an aggressive plan to gain some counterplay on the queenside.

| | 14 | ... | ♘h6 |
| | 15 | ♖a3 | 0-0-0 |

A bold decision, declaring total war against the white king. Instead 15 ... 0-0 would be quite level. Now a fierce race develops on opposite wings.

What should White play now?

16 a5?!

150 points, but this advance is really too reckless and the safer 16 ♘f3 instead earns *200 points*.

	16	...	h4
	17	a6	b6
	18	♘f3	hxg3
	19	fxg3	f6

A difficult move is coming now. What can it be?

20 c5!!

500 points. An inspired sacrifice which Kasparov claimed was necessary to maintain fighting chances. It is a measure of the extreme difficulty of this game that when he played the sacrifice Kasparov had a mere six minutes left to complete his next twenty moves in order to avoid losing by time forfeit.

20 ...   dxc5

Not 20 ... bxc5 when White can swiftly penetrate the black fortress with 21 ♖b3 followed by ♖b7.

What is the best move now to justify the sacrifice?

21 ♕b3

400 points. Think carefully about Black's best response and the details involved. A large bonus is coming.

21 ...   ♔b8?

This move is too cautious and allows Kasparov to build up the attack he has been dreaming of for so long. Correct, and guaranteeing Black some advantage, is 21 ... ♘g4 22 ♘xg4 ♕xg4 23 ♕f7 ♖h7 24 ♕xe7 ♗h8! and Black wins. Kasparov said he would have played 24 h4 which is met by 24 ... ♕d7 when Black can start to consolidate. Award yourself *400 bonus points* if you saw the variation ending in 24 ... ♗h8!

22	♖d1	♕c8
23	♘c4	♖xd1
24	♕xd1	♘f7
25	♖d3	g5
26	♕b3	

If 26 ♖d7 ♖d8 repels boarders.

26	...	♕e6
27	♗e3	♘c8

Most players would have contented themselves with 28 ♗xc5. Kasparov, with both players on the precipice of losing by time forfeit, finds a fresh way to hurl the position into utter confusion. What is it?

28 ♘xb6!!

500 points. A brilliant solution.

28	...	♛xb3
29	♘d7+	♚c7
30	♖xb3	♚xd7
31	♖b7+	♚e6
32	♗xc5	♗f8

This was the only move.

33	♘d4+	♚e5
34	♘xc6+	♚xe4
35	♗xa7	♘fd6
36	♖c7	♘xa7
37	♖xa7	♘c4
38	♖a8	♗g7
39	♖a7	

Think now about Black's best defence in this difficult endgame.

39	...	♘e3+

In the scramble to make forty moves Nigel Short overlooks that the simple 39 ... ♗f8 leaves White with nothing better than to steer for draw with 40 ♖a8 repeating the position. The text distances Black's knight from White's dangerous passed a-pawn. If you saw this give yourself *250 bonus points.*

40	♔g1	♖g8
41	♖e7+	

Consider now whether Black can still manage to save himself.

41	...	♔d3

So great was the confusion after the rush to reach the time control that the tournament officials here erroneously announced that Black had lost on time, a statement which they soon had to retract. Nevertheless, Black's 41st is the losing error after which he can no longer prevent the coronation of White's a-pawn. 41 ... ♔d5 would have retained drawing chances. *200 bonus points* if you saw this.

42	a7	♖c8
43	♔f2	♘d1+
44	♔f3	g4+
45	♔xg4	f5+
46	♔f3	♗xb2
47	♖d7+	♔c2
48	♖d8	1-0

You should keep a record of your points scored on the table below so that you can add them up at the end of this book and calculate your exact chess strength.

Your points for this game.
Tick one of these:

2800 ☐
2700+ ☐
2600+ ☐
2500+ ☐
2400+ ☐
2300+ ☐
2200+ ☐

2000+ ☐
1800+ ☐
1600+ ☐
1400+ ☐
1200+ ☐
1000+ ☐
less than 1000 ☐

Conclusion

Now that you have reached the end of this book I suggest that you go back through the records you have kept and add up the total number of points you have scored. Divide that total by 20 (the number of games in this book) to obtain your average and you will now have a much clearer insight into the potential of your chess strength and the rating that you should be able to achieve. If you have been following this book closely, your points score per game should have been increasing steadily throughout the book. Use the self-improvement graph on page 8 to find out whether this has been the case.

Final strength table

If your average over the 25 games was:

2500+	you have the potential to become a grandmaster
2400+	you have the potential to become an international master
2300+	you have the potential to become a FIDE master
2200+	you have the potential to become a national master
2000+	you have the potential to achieve a published FIDE-rating
1800+	you have the potential to become a strong club player
1600+	you should already be a club player
1400+	you should be able to give your home computer a good game
1200+	you play well, but can advance further
1000+	you have some experience, but there is much scope for improvement
1000–	keep reading *The Times* chess column for further practice

Raymond Keene